Letters to My Daughter

Letters to My Daughter

The story of how one family overcame tragedy and loss

TIM ORR

ISBN: 1979534217
ISBN 13: 9781979534215
Library of Congress Control Number: 2017917532
CreateSpace Independent Publishing Platform
North Charleston, South Carolina

Table of Contents

Forward

I first met Michelle Orr in May of 2014 at the transition case conference for her daughter, Faith, who would be attending Taylorsville Elementary that fall as a kindergarten student. From the moment we made introductions and Michelle introduced herself as Faith's mother, I knew a much deeper connection existed than just Mother-Daughter.

As a teacher at Columbus Signature Academy - New Tech High School, one of three high schools serving the students of our community, Michelle's responsibilities prevented us from interacting as frequently as we did with her husband and Faith's dad, Tim, but I felt her impact in each conversation with Faith. It was during her first year at Taylorsville that Tim wrote his first book, *We Named Her Faith*, and I had the unique opportunity to read portions of this as he was writing it. It was here that I learned the Orr Family story.

As our friendship with the Orr family grew, we enjoyed several excursions in which I was able to interact with Michelle, Tim, and Faith on a more personal level, and I truly was in awe of the commitment Michelle and Tim had to Faith. Their faith in God had given them this precious gift, and even her name reflected their undying love and trust that He would protect them through any situation.

That very faith was tested repeatedly in 2016 when we prayed with this family for Michelle's healing following a diagnosis of cancer. Claiming her healing in late spring, the family embarked on a memorable trip to Disney World, not knowing that this would be one of the last times they would create lasting memories with Michelle. For on June 27, 2016, Michelle's passed away while in Michigan visiting family.

How does a mother's legacy live on? How does a father continue to honor his child's name when the very core of his existence is tested? How does a child remember the parent without the grief overwhelming her mind? I answer with two scriptures from *The Holy Bible*, Mark 11:22: Have faith in God. Luke 1:37: For with God nothing shall be impossible.

Tim and Faith remind us all that, even in the darkest hour of our days, we can be assured that God is making a way for us when we have *faith*!

Principal Sydell Gant
Taylorsville Elementary School

Preface

I am sure you have heard the rags to riches story of the guy who grows up in a broken home and later becomes an alcoholic. Then, when he is at the end of his rope, he has a religious conversion that turns his life around. He lives the rest of his life experiencing the American Dream. He loves his job, marries the woman of his dreams, and adopts the daughter he always wanted. That was the story I told in my first book, *We Named Her Faith*.[1]

I expected to write another book someday in which I would continue the story by showing how our daughter, Faith, grew up to be a fine young woman. And I still plan to write that book.

But the story I tell in *this* book is not that story. The happy, successful life I enjoyed, with the family I always wanted, has given way to an unexpected new chapter.

No author writes alone. There are always people who come alongside to assist in some capacity that propels the writer forward. Such people are worthy of acknowledgment.

The first one I want to acknowledge is my late wife, Michelle. We were married for 23 years before her untimely death. She was my best friend, and I miss her. She was the one who first encouraged me to be a writer.

---

1 Tim Orr. *We Named Her Faith: How We Became a Gospel-centered Family*. (Maitland, FL: Xulon Press, 2015).

The second person on my list is Faith. I am so thankful for the opportunity to be her father, and to tell her story. She makes my day ... every day. I have learned more from her than she has from me.

Third, I want to thank Terrace Lake Church, which has stood by me through all the difficult experiences over the last two years, and for the elders, with whom I have served over the years. You have impacted me to be more like Christ.

Fourth, I offer special thanks to Taylorsville Elementary School, led by Principal Sydell Gant. You all are amazing. I couldn't ask for a better school for my daughter. Your love and concern for Faith will never be forgotten.

Last, thank you to Help at Home for taking care of Faith the way you do. Your commitment to reading to her, tutoring, and engaging with her in one-on-one play, duties that Michelle once filled, has made a great impact on Faith. It has also allowed me to write this book.

Before you plunge into the book, I think I need to answer the following question: Why the title, *Letters to My Daughter*? As you read, you'll notice that the letters to Faith don't appear until much later in the book. Before I share them, I want to show you what happened that prompted the letters.

I pray that this book will inspire you to be the person that God wants you to be, no matter what. As Max Lucado has pointed out, "God never said that the journey would be easy, but He did say that the arrival would be worthwhile."[2]

I would like to invite you to journey with me as I explain how God helped me and my daughter overcome an incredible tragedy and turned it into something beautiful.

---

2 Max Lucado, *In the Eye of the Storm: Jesus Knows How You Feel* (Nashville: Thomas Nelson, 1991), 84.

One

My Life's Journey

In 1968, when I was developing in my mother's womb, technology had not yet advanced so that anyone saw my birth defects coming. After a long and difficult labor, my mom gave birth to a son with multiple birth defects. Me.

At first, the doctors and nurses let Mom rest and didn't show me to her. She spent all night not knowing what happened to me. She lay in her bed wondering if I was okay and what I looked like.

The next day, to prepare my mother for the surprise, they brought her pictures of me. They showed her first-born son with a cleft lip, cleft palate, and webbed fingers. After digesting this news, my mother, bless her, welcomed me with open arms.

During my next 17 years, I spent a lot of time at Riley Hospital. I saw a level of human suffering from which most kids my age were shielded. Because many of my operations required skin grafts, I was usually sent to the burn unit, where the nurses were best equipped to tend to my needs. Normally I spent a week or so there to heal after my surgeries. I witnessed many kids enduring agony.

Other difficult experiences shaped my life me during this time. My father's alcoholism marital infidelity, and rage were regular features of our home life. My dad beat up my mom, often leaving her face black and blue. It was nothing to see him drunk, even driving us home while drunk. We were not allowed to object. He was in total control. When I was 5, my mom had had enough and filed for divorce.

As a 5-year-old, I was trying to deal with the trauma of surgeries and the consequences that go along with them. My parents' divorce hit me hard, as I had no sense of security in my life. I lacked the secure environment that comes when both parents are present. My mom did her best, but she was saddled with her own problems.

By the age of 15, I was hurting and consumed by self-loathing, anger, and rebellion. The years of childhood trauma had taken their toll.

I took my first drink at a friend's house on a cold winter's Saturday afternoon. We were talking in his room when my friend Troy suggested that we go downstairs to the liquor cabinet. I liked the idea, so down we went. He poured the vodka and lemonade, and I drank the enticing mixture. Suddenly the pain, anger, and bitterness from my life of rejection vanished.

That same year I began to battle with suicidal thoughts. From the time I was 15 until my conversion, I contemplated suicide almost daily. During my senior year of high school while I was living with a friend, I went so far as to put the barrel of a gun to my temple. Thank God, that's as far as it went.

At 21, the trajectory of my life dramatically changed when I converted to Christianity. It wasn't that I no longer had issues. It was just that now I could have the victory over them if I surrendered those areas of my life to Christ. Acquiring victory in the weak areas of my life drove me to go deeper and deeper in my understanding of the gospel. Fear also melted from my heart. I began to understand how much God loved me. I realized I didn't have to earn His approval. He was no longer the traffic cop in the sky, waiting to punish me. Instead, God became my loving Heavenly Father. The more that I understood how much I had been forgiven, the more I understood His love, which allowed me to grow in my understanding of His grace.

Just two years after my conversion, I found myself sitting in chapel at a Christian college, listening to a sermon. The speaker, referring to the Book of Joel, told us that if we would seek God and put Him first, God would restore everything the locusts of sin had eaten. I took this as a promise that one day, I, too, would live out the American Dream, which, for me, consisted of having a wife and kids. I had believed that past sins had robbed me of the security of a healthy, loving family. Now, I thought, God was promising me one. Two years later, God put Michelle and me together. There could not have been a better match for me.

It took 16 years after I married Michelle until the promise was completely fulfilled. On July 17, 2009, Michelle and I adopted our daughter, Faith, an incredible blessing who was born with Down syndrome.

For six years, I lived out my version of the American Dream. Then one day, my life suddenly became a nightmare. My assumption that I would finish with a happy, successful life, complete with the family I always wanted, turned out to be a mirage. As this book unfolds, you will discover the beautiful family that God brought together and the tragedy that broke us apart. You will get an unvarnished, behind the scenes look at our experience and how we processed and eventually overcame this tragedy.

Two

The Lessons of Horatio

Before I tell you more of my own story of suffering, I'd like to tell you about Horatio Spafford. He was a prominent Chicago lawyer, yet he was a man of many sorrows, too.

In October 1871, the Great Chicago Fire killed more than 250 of his neighbors and left tens of thousands homeless. Horatio's family experienced great financial loss from the fire. Yet Horatio and his wife helped many people put their lives back together, despite the tremendous adversity visited upon them.

That would not be the only devastation for the Spaffords. In 1873, Horatio and his family decided to vacation in England. Because of his work, Horatio couldn't leave immediately with his family. So he stayed home to wrap up some things at work, planning to join them shortly. Horatio's wife and four kids went ahead of him on a transatlantic voyage.

While at home working, Horatio received the news that their ship had sunk after colliding with another vessel. The next day, another ship arrived, rescuing some of the passengers. Unfortunately, Horatio's daughters were not among them. Horatio's wife sent her husband a telegraph that said she was "saved alone."

After hearing the news, Horatio boarded a ship to be with his wife. As the ship traversed the area where the doomed vessel sank, the Chicago attorney penned the classic hymn *It is Well with My Soul.* It reveals the depth of his Christian faith, which fostered a strength that was "bathed in hope."[3] This first verse captures this idea quite well.

When peace like a river attendeth my way,
When sorrows like sea-billows roll,
Whatever my lot, Thou has taught me to know:
"It is well, it is well with my soul."

After losing four daughters, what would give Horatio peace like a river? What were the resources available to him? The hymn reveals that his faith was more than mere creedal commitments of a nominal churchgoer. Horatio had a vibrant faith that was both informed theologically and experienced practically. A closer look at this hymn reveals the beliefs that sustained Horatio through his suffering, namely his beliefs about creation, God, the world, salvation, and Jesus, all resources that helped him respond to tragedy.

Creation

Most Christians would have been devastated by this kind of experience. Yet Horatio's belief in the fallenness of the world helped him to understand suffering and misfortune. "The doctrine of the Fall" gave him "a remarkably nuanced understanding of suffering" because it answered the *why* question of suffering.[4]

The Christian creation story begins with God creating the world out of nothing. Prior to his creation, there wasn't just empty space, because space had yet to be created. Creation was good because sin had not yet

---

3 Timothy Keller, *Walking with God through Pain and Suffering* (New York: Penguin Publishing Group, 2013), Kindle Location 736.
4 Keller, Kindle Location 1828-1829.

infected the world. No poverty, no tsunamis, no hurricanes, no sin, no evil, and no death. Everything was perfect.

Then followed the Fall, which came by way of the serpent, who deceived Adam and Eve about God's command. God told them they could eat of any tree in the garden except the tree of the knowledge of good and evil. The serpent, however, challenged God's rule by distorting His command. Tragically, Adam and Eve succumbed to the temptation.

Therefore, the entire human race has suffered the consequences. Adam and Eve were suddenly separated from God, having forfeited the close fellowship with Him they had enjoyed. Thus, "… the good pattern of the life God created … now falls far short of its original intent," making alienation, fear, guilt, and shame to be felt by all mankind.[5] "Because we rejected his authority everything about the world—our hearts, emotions, bodies, our relationships to other people, and our relationship to nature itself—stopped working as it should."[6] Even today, both the world and humanity are broken.

How does this doctrine relate to Horatio's plight? He understood that he was not promised a problem-free life and that tragedies befall both the just and the unjust (Matt. 5:45). Christian "teaching rejects the idea that people who suffer more are always worse people than those who suffer less."[7] Horatio saw his situation as the result of living in a fallen world. He didn't expect God to give him a perfect life. This Christian realism helped Horatio to in his devastating experience.

The Renewal of the World

Horatio understood that although we live in a fallen world, he also knew that it would one day be renewed.

He also must have understood the promise that when Jesus returns to establish a new heaven and a new earth, He "will wipe away every tear from their eyes, and death shall be no more, neither shall there be

---

5 Keller, Kindle Location 1826-1827.

6 Keller, Kindle Location 1822-1824).

7 Keller, Kindle Location 1829-1830.

mourning, nor crying, nor pain anymore, for the former things have passed away" (Rev. 21:4). This renewal is possible because of what Jesus did on the cross two millennia ago. "The cross secured the defeat of evil in the past, on Calvary, but now it also guarantees a final experience of that defeat in the future, in the renewal of all things, when every tear will be wiped away."[8] While still living on earth, believers are to wait for the coming renewal of all things, patiently.

In Romans 8:18-30, Paul shows how the suffering we endure here pales in comparison with the glory believers will receive when the world is renewed. Hence, we can focus on the final reward of the faith, even in the face of seemingly impossible circumstances. When Paul refers to "all things" working together for out good, he means "that the 'all things' we are guaranteed because of Christ's death for us includes both our final glory and all that God provides to bring us to that glory (see the "good" of Rom. 8:28)."[9] The last stanza of the song reads:

But, Lord, 'tis for Thee, for Thy coming we wait,
The sky, not the grave, is our goal;
Oh, trump of the angel! Oh, voice of the Lord!
Blessed hope, blessed rest of my soul!

And Lord, haste the day when the faith shall be sight,
The clouds be rolled back as a scroll;
The trump shall resound, and the Lord shall descend,
Even so, it is well with my soul.

Clearly, Horatio understood that the world was not what God intended it to be, but would not remain in that state. We live during the period between the first two chapters of the Bible (Gen. 1-2), which spell out the perfection of God's original creation, and the last two chapters of

8 Keller, Kindle Locations 2520-2521.
9 Douglas J. Moo, Romans *The NIV Application Commentary Book 6,* (Grand Rapids: Zondervan Publishing House, 2009). Kindle Locations 6137-6139.

the Bible (Rev. 20-21), which speak of its renewal. For now, the world is fallen, so "we groan inwardly" as we endure the pains that this life brings. Yet, at the same time, we "wait eagerly for [our] adoption as sons, [and] the redemption of our bodies" (Rom. 8:23).

Romans 8:18-30 outlines the future renewed world that believers will inhabit and encourages us to wait patiently for it (Rom. 8:18-25). Because of this glorious future, we can endure the suffering we experience in this life because it pales in comparison with what we will receive in the next.

This perspective goes against a secular worldview, which sees "suffering as an interruption of the freedom that makes you happiest,"[10] which says there is no reality beyond this world. When people die, according to secularism, they cease to exist. There is no hope beyond this life.

Paul, however, thinks otherwise. He shows that God has provided what we need in this life as we await a glorious future (Rom. 8:25-30). God has given believers "the Holy Spirit" who "plays a crucial role as the 'bridge' between our present experience as God's children and our final adoption into his family."[11] The Spirit intercedes for us in our suffering.

God's Plan for Believers in this World

Horatio also believed in God's sovereignty, His absolute rule over the world. God directs the affairs of people in all aspects of their lives, as well as the affairs of nations, and the rest of His created order. Nothing happens without God's consent (while still allowing people to have free will, a doctrine known as compatibilism).

The Apostle Paul instructs us to consider how God can use everything, including suffering, for our good. He encouraged the church at Rome to rejoice in their sufferings because it produced "endurance," "character," and "hope." The bonus for Christians is that God has not

---

10 Keller, Kindle Locations 2988-2989.
11 Moo, Kindle Locations 5747-5749.

left us alone to face this difficult task. He has given us the Holy Spirit, who has been poured out in our hearts (Rom. 5:3-5).

Though Horatio lost his four children, the sovereignty of God was obvious to him as he reflected on how his wife was spared. "Fortunately, a sailor rowing a small boat around that area spotted a woman floating on a piece of the wreckage. It was Anna. Anna was pulled into the boat and later picked up by another large vessel which landed in Cardiff, Wales nine days later."[12] Of the many questions he was tempted to ask, the first one, I am sure, was, *if God had allowed his wife to be saved, why didn't He save his kids?* Yet, the first verse of the song records the response of a man who resisted any doubts in God's sovereignty. "Whatever my lot, thou hast taught me to say, it is well, it is well with my soul." The soul of a man who finds peace during a tragedy like this is the soul of a man who truly trusts God with everything.

The Assurance of Salvation

The assurance of Horatio's salvation is the anchor that allows all the other truths already mentioned to take root.

Though Satan should buffet, though trials should come,
Let this blest assurance control,
That Christ hath regarded my helpless estate,
And hath shed His own blood for my soul.

My sin—oh, the bliss of this glorious thought!
My sin, not in part but the whole,
Is nailed to the cross, and I bear it no more,
Praise the Lord, praise the Lord, O my soul!

---

12 Jonathan Tristan, *Top 10 Wonderful Stories Behind Christian Hymns: The 10 most amazing and Inspirational stories that will help you uplift your spirit and faith* (Amazon Digital Services, 2017), 4.

For me, be it Christ, be it Christ hence to live:
If Jordan above me shall roll,
No pang shall be mine, for in death as in life
Thou wilt whisper Thy peace to my soul.

Horatio wanted to let the assurance of his salvation control his response to this situation. It caused him to rejoice in the face of normally unbearable circumstances. Tim Keller says that, because of the finished work of Christ, believers "are assured that the difficulties of life are not payment for our past sins, since Jesus has paid for them. As Luther taught, suffering is unbearable if you aren't certain that God is for you and with you."[13] It was this assurance that whispered peace to Horatio's soul.

This assurance has brought peace to mine, as well.

---

13 Keller, Kindle Locations 974-981.

Three

Our Love Story

J ohn Green, author of *The Fault in Our Stars,* said, "I will not tell you our love story, because—like all real love stories—it will die with us, as it should."[14] I couldn't disagree more. Love stories should be told over and over because they bring encouragement and showcase what loving relationships between two people can look like.

We live in a broken world, where relationships are disposable. In this environment, it's easy to think that a happy marriage is impossible. A good love story, however, can restore hope.

Our love story began in a very different way than many you hear of today. Too often, these days, people meet a stranger online, get to know them first through emails and phone calls, before finally going on the first date.

Michelle and I knew each other for two years before our first date. We met at church during the fall of 1990, shortly after she arrived in Marshall, a small Illinois town near my residence of Terre Haute, Indiana. The year before, after graduating from Central Michigan University she had started her teaching career in the Houston area but decided that

---

14 John Green, *The Fault in Our Stars* (New York: Dutton Books, 2012), quoted at https://www.goodreads.com/quotes/491033-i-will-not-tell-you-our-love-story-because-like-all.

the distance between Texas and her home state of Michigan was too great. So she took a position in Marshall, about 20 minutes from Terre Haute. Marshall, a small country town in Illinois, didn't include a church in her preferred denomination, so she ventured over to Terre Haute to find one.

When I say Michelle and I met at the church, we were more like acquaintances. We rarely interacted, but when we did it never rose above mere small talk.

I was a recent convert to Christianity, from a life ravaged by alcoholism. I was carrying a lot of baggage and needed to change a lot of things in my life. Socially awkward, I didn't interact with people much at church. I remember being terrified to talk to anyone. Often, I sat in a pew toward the back of the church until the service started, hoping someone would talk with me. Invariably, someone would.

This social awkwardness was nothing new. Before my conversion, I needed to have a drink to be able to function socially. After I came to Christ, it took a few years to start feeling somewhat comfortable interacting with people I didn't know very well. I especially didn't feel comfortable interacting with the opposite sex. So, obviously, Michelle and I didn't talk much.

The First Date

Then in May 1992, things took a radical turn. Michelle decided to ask me out. I was glad she did, since I had only been on one date since my conversion three years earlier. She didn't ask me straight out. Instead, she opted to ask her friend, who then asked the pastor's wife to ask the pastor if I would go out with her. While her actions violated every accepted dating procedure imaginable, they worked. I returned a "yes" back through that chain of communication.

When we went on our first date, once again, Michelle defied the conventional way and picked me up. This wasn't because she had no regard for gender roles. The reason was simple: I did not have a driver's license. A few years earlier, I had been arrested for the third time for driving while intoxicated, consumption by a minor, and reckless driving. Since I had failed to do what was required to get my license back, I was still without one. Michelle knew I didn't have a car but didn't realize I had no license until we left the house for our date. As we walked out to the car, Michelle asked if I would drive. She came from a family where the men always drove.

I reluctantly told her I didn't have my license and she would have to do the driving. The look on her face was priceless! Her disbelief, dismay, and even fear were evident. Years later, she told me that she doubted our relationship would go anywhere at that point.

Despite the rocky start, however, the date went quite well. We went to the *Olive Garden* for dinner. I was nervous, not knowing what exactly to say. But the words seemed to come when I needed them, and we enjoyed nice, polite conversation and began to get to know each other.

Then we decided to go play miniature golf, engaging in small talk the entire time. Since we hadn't talked much nearly the entire two years we knew one another, we had a lot to talk about. Michelle told me where she grew up and what it was like to be a Michigander. I, in turn, shared with her my mischievous past, difficult childhood, and my dreams for ministry. We capped off the night on a Ferris wheel at the Banks of the Wabash Festival.

Despite the romantic evening, that night I decided this would be my first and last date with Michelle. I had determined that my future wife was back at Lee College, now Lee University, where I had just finished my first year. My sights were set on finding a wife there.

Courtship and Marriage

After our date, Michelle went back to Michigan, where she would spend the summer with her parents. During those two months, Michelle felt a clear leading from God that she was getting married soon. She was so sure that marriage loomed on the horizon that she began to plan the wedding. She picked out the wedding colors and decided where the wedding would be located among other details. Several months later, when we decided to get married, her planning made it very easy for me. All of the important decisions had already been made!

While Michelle wasn't sure if I was the one she would marry, I was sure that she *wasn't* the one for me. I needed to be persuaded. So everyone, from my closest friends to my pastor, took it upon themselves to tell me Michelle was the one. But because I was preparing for vocational ministry, I assumed I would meet my wife at Lee College. It only made sense. I was relying on my own understanding at that point.

When Michelle returned from summer break a few months later, I saw her at church. I don't remember much of the pastor's message. I do, however, remember the altar call, at least the Holy Spirit's leading. I felt an overwhelming confirmation in my heart that I was to marry Michelle. In hindsight, I wouldn't recommend choosing a spouse this way, but given my problems and spiritual immaturity, God chose sovereignly to work in this way.

Immediately after the service, I made a beeline over to Michelle and asked her out. She graciously accepted, with her mother and grandmother listening in on our conversation. When I left, they both said to Michelle, "Who is he?" I had no idea that I would be Michelle's husband in a little under a year. My request for a date turned out to be the beginning of a wonderful 10-month courtship.

Marriage Bells Are Ringing

Since I had seen so much divorce, hurt, and pain over the years, I was determined to have a great marriage and family. To prepare, Michelle and I went through three or four marriage books as well as six weeks of premarital counseling with our pastor. I wanted no stone left unturned. Together we prayed, fasted, talked, and discussed every facet of marriage, ranging from sex to finances. We tried to do everything we could to prepare for a happy marriage and glean the wisdom necessary to be parents. We pictured our future as having the typical two wonderful kids and living in a house with the proverbial white picket fence.

On June 12, 1993, Michelle and I exchanged our wedding vows. The ceremony was in a quaint little town called Barryton, Michigan, about 40 minutes from Mount Pleasant, the nearest larger town. Most of Michelle's family was there, and some of my family made the eight-hour trip. Our pastor, Randy Ballard, presided. The church, Michelle's home congregation, was nearly full.

Since neither of us made much money at the time, it was a frugal affair. To drastically cut costs, the church graciously catered the wedding. Several ladies from the church cooked a wonderful meal. Michelle's mom baked the wedding cake to perfection. The wedding dress was homemade, again by her mother, but looked like something one would buy at an upscale establishment. We felt blessed.

At the reception, I was engaging in small talk with Michelle when I suddenly noticed several people tapping their glasses with their spoons. I leaned over and asked Michelle what these countrified people were doing. She informed me that this was a longstanding tradition: cueing the groom to kiss the bride. Each spouse comes to a marriage with longstanding traditions. I was happy to be getting my first lesson in Michelle's.

Many people that day sensed that God had His hand on our marriage. In hindsight, they were right. Looking back almost 24 years since that day, I am convinced I married the right person. During our 23-year marriage, Michelle and I grew very close and became best friends.

But I don't want to convey that we had a storybook marriage. There is no such thing as a perfect marriage. When two sinful people come together, there is bound to be conflict along the way, and our union was no exception. Thank God, the strategies we established during our courtship helped to resolve discord when it emerged.

While there are no perfect marriages, there are good ones and bad ones. That day was the start of a good one. Having done earnestly all we could do to prepare, we trusted God to do the rest. He didn't disappoint. God was there when we called to Him, walked with us through the storms, and guided us to establish, not a storybook marriage, but a very happy one.

Of course, no marriage is complete without a honeymoon. Since neither of us had much money, we planned to spend a couple days at nearby Indiana Beach then return to work after a couple of days. Indiana Beach is an amusement park located on beautiful Lake Shafer in Monticello, Indiana, about three hours southeast from Barryton. Unfortunately, the forecast called for storms that week, which rained out our honeymoon. What were we to do?

At the time, I was an aspiring young pastor in training, so I thought it would be a good idea to spend our honeymoon at a camp meeting put on by my grandmother's denomination. Yes, you read that last sentence correctly, and Michelle didn't complain. We spent our honeymoon attending workshops during the day and enjoying the evening service at night.

During one of the evening sessions, Michelle and I introduced ourselves to some of the people sitting nearby. After exchanging a few pleasantries, I told one gentleman we were on our honeymoon. I will never forget the look on his face as he promptly replied, "Then, what are you doing here?" I shot a quick glance at Michelle and got the stomach-churning suspicion that she might be thinking the same thing. I realized that this was not how she had envisioned her honeymoon. It took me a couple trips to *Disney World* later in our marriage to make up for my mistake—which allowed Mickey Mouse to serve a redemptive purpose!

Would We Have Kids?

Kids, I believe, are not essential to a happy marriage. One can be perfectly happy while remaining childless. However, this truth failed to provide any comfort for Michelle and me. Early in our marriage, after trying unsuccessfully to get the process going, we wondered whether she couldn't have children due to a longstanding thyroid condition. So we decided to visit the doctor.

We both walked into his office nervously. I wasn't sure if I wanted a definitive answer to our question about fertility. Not knowing any specifics about a possible problem allowed me to hope that one day we would have a child of our own. Michelle felt the same way.

After undergoing the necessary tests, Michelle and I sat in the doctor's office waiting to hear the results. When the doctor entered, he provided no facial expression that would clue us in. He sat down, eased back in his chair, opened the file, and stoically relayed to us the test results. Michelle's suspicions were confirmed. It would be very unlikely that she could bear children. The door of opportunity to have children had been, it seemed, forcefully slammed shut.

Conclusion

Early in our marriage, our dream to have children was crushed. I had envisioned taking a son to baseball practice and pouring my heart into him so he could be the husband and father God intended him to be. I also envisioned taking my daughter to dance recitals, assisting my wife in hosting slumber parties or, at least, being in the other room as my wife assumed the honors. Then, finally one day I would walk "my little girl" down the aisle so she could marry the man of her dreams. Now we figured that these dreams would elude us.

We soon learned how to stuff our pain through doing ministry and building careers. For a while, our busy lives distracted us from a gnawing sense of loss.

Four

WE DECIDE TO ADOPT

Several years passed after Michelle and I found out that we couldn't have kids biologically. Though we suppressed our feelings, our hearts still yearned for a child. Then, roughly around the summer of 2008, we began the process of adopting a child. It began as a half-hearted attempt. We didn't really know what direction to take. Did we really want a newborn as we began our 40s? Could we really afford adoption? While we never allowed the doubts and questions to dominate our thinking, they persisted. However, our desire for one last chance to pour our lives into someone else's life was greater than our doubts.

Michelle and I launched ourselves into the adoption process. Paperwork, interviews, and observations abounded. What kind of baby were we willing to adopt? Would a child with a different cultural heritage be OK? Does the age of the child matter? How about disabilities? While the questions made us uncomfortable at first, we knew they were an essential part of the process. After all, the adoption agency needed to know if a prospective child was a right fit for the adoptive family.

We were open to any race or nationality. Given our extensive multicultural experiences, this was a "no brainer." Concerning age, we wanted a newborn. As Brooke, our adoption coordinator, reviewed the list of possibilities, she asked us about disabilities. Because of our age, we decided against adopting a child with special needs. We learned later, however, that God had other plans.

Christmastime

Michelle and I made our way to my mom's to celebrate Christmas with my side of the family. My mother, grandmother, sister, and both brothers were in the living room waiting for everyone to arrive. As was our tradition, Mom, my sister, and my grandmother finished preparing the meal. Then everyone gathered around the table, followed by our exchange of gifts.

I noticed a somber look on Michelle's face. I thought nothing of it, not realizing she was a little depressed because of yet another childless Christmas.

Sometimes these kinds of experiences either drive us to despair or drive us to God. For Michelle, it was the latter. On our way home, she wanted us to pray together and voice our concerns to God. When she prayed, she told God how much she wanted a child.

As we continued to make our way home, Michelle kept praying, but silently, unbeknownst to me, in the passenger's seat. In the middle of her prayer, she later said she felt a confirmation from God that we would have a child of our own before Christmas next year. It seemed far-fetched, even to her, but she felt an assurance that was unexplainable. When she got home, she wrote of her experience in her adoption journal and forgot about it.

God Changes Our Plans

We were several months into the adoption process, yet we had no clear direction. Would we choose a newborn or adopt a toddler? Would it be a domestic or an international adoption? Girl or a boy? Around April 2009, Michelle again suggested we take some time for extended prayer on one of our trips to Michigan. As she prayed, Michelle once again felt impressed by the Holy Spirit that we would have a child that year.

In May, we received clear direction. I was teaching a religion course at the local university and, whenever I could, doing substitute teaching during the day to supplement our income. The evening before the first day of a two-day assignment at a local elementary school, I was ill and unable to go into work. Normally, if a substitute doesn't show up on the first day of a two-day assignment, the school will find someone else to teach the second day. Fortunately, it allowed me to come to work and teach the class on that second day.

I was told my assignment was to teach the preschool special needs class, an age group with which I am not particularly gifted. Even though one of my graduate degrees is in elementary education, the university never taught me how to teach 3-year-olds. Teaching adults at the university level was much more my forte.

When the students got off the bus and entered the classroom, a little girl named Lydia immediately walked up and tilted her head to look at the tall man in front of her. When she did, she extended her arms straight up, the universal sign to get picked up. I obliged. We walked around the room a bit, pointing out things and discussing what they were. Then I put her down. She walked away, only briefly, to return and asked me to pick her up again. When I did, something happened inside of me. I felt a leading from the Holy Spirit to adopt a child with Down syndrome, which I had not considered before.

Later that day, my doubts got the best of me as I began to think about the possible challenges. I talked to both teacher's assistants that day. They informed me of the issues I might face. Despite the doubts, I decided to run my thoughts by Michelle. We were down to one car, so I had to pick her up.

When I arrived at her school, she got into the car and began to tell me about her day. When there was a pause in the conversation, I shared what had happened in my classroom. I told her I thought God might be leading us to adopt a child with Down syndrome. I expected Michelle to say something like, "We really need to think this through." Instead, she told me that my words had witnessed to her. She encouraged me to consider the matter further.

A Phone Call Away

I began by contacting the Department of Child and Family Services, asking if there were any children with Down syndrome who needed a home. The lady said she had been in her position for several years and had never heard of a child with that disability being put up for adoption through her agency. She encouraged me to check with other, more specialized adoption agencies.

I contacted the Down Syndrome Association of Greater Cincinnati, which seeks to educate people so that they will keep their children born with Down syndrome. The association also helps set up possible adoption relationships. It connected us with a wonderful lady named Robin Steele. Robin is the founder of the National Down Syndrome Adoption Network. Besides adopting her own children with Down syndrome, she has matched many children to adoptive families.

The Adoption Process Begins

As we talked over the phone one afternoon, I could hear the excitement in Robin's voice as she learned that my wife and I wanted to adopt a child with Down syndrome. Robin told me that there happened to be a family in Indiana that wanted to place a child for adoption once the baby was born. However, there were a few caveats. The birth family wanted a family that had no other children in the home and who desired an open adoption.

In an open adoption, the adoptive family and birth family maintain a cordial relationship that includes face-to-face visits and open contact via phone, email, and so on. I was hesitant. I feared that Michelle and I might be taken advantage of or have our privacy violated. I asked about the family, and Robin calmed my fears. The birth family was excellent and just wanted the best for their daughter. She asked if we wanted to pursue the adoption. With a sense of relief, I replied with an emphatic "Yes!"

Robin said that the birth family had had a few inquiries already but didn't think any of the prospective parents were a good fit. My initial thought was that since Michelle and I were in our 40s, they might think we were not the right fit, either. But those doubts did not deter us. We knew God had a plan for our family.

Robin explained that our next step was to send the family a birth letter about who we are and why we want to adopt. We knew we would probably hear back soon. The birth mother was late into her pregnancy and wanted to place her child for adoption as soon as she was born.

A few days later, Michelle and I emailed Robin our letter, and she forwarded it to the family. We patiently waited for a response. Many of our Christian friends were notified as well, as we asked them to pray for us. After a week or two, we assumed that the birth parents weren't interested. But shortly thereafter, we discovered they *were* interested!

The next step was a conference call. We set up a time and anxiously waited. When we finally got the call, Michelle and I huddled around our cell phone with the speaker on. After some small talk, the couple told us some of the issues the baby might face. There were possible heart issues and probably a blocked intestine that would need to be taken care of right after birth.

Then the husband shared that he had a phobia of medical issues and could not handle this diagnosis. Michelle and I will never forget him saying, "We didn't understand why God would do this, but we knew that someone must have been praying for a child, and God knew we would never abort our child."

After this conversation, we learned that the couple wanted to meet us. The arrangements were made for a visit in about a week. The waiting was difficult, yet an increasing assurance arose in me that everything was in God's hand, and that He had a plan. Michelle and I spent each night praying that God would open this door.

Finally, when the birth family visited us on a Saturday, it was like we had known one another all our lives. We had so much in common. The birth father and I were both politically conservative and fervent IU basketball and Bobby Knight fans, for example. As we continued our conversation, I could sense that this was really going to happen. God was going to give us a daughter. When our meeting wrapped up a few hours later, I could see from Michelle's expression how excited she was. We were hopeful we would hear good news right away.

On the first Sunday after our meeting, I went to the altar asked the pastor and his wife pray for us. The burden to pray had overwhelmed me, and I began sobbing, almost uncontrollably. The Holy Spirit gave me an incredible assurance that we would have a daughter soon. Michelle, kneeling right next to me, felt the same way.

A few days later, we received a call from the birth family asking if we were willing to raise their daughter as our own. We had to restrain ourselves from bellowing out our excitement, but when we hung up, we jumped for joy, holding one another tightly. What I had been promised in the college chapel 17 years ago that God would return everything the locusts had eaten had been fulfilled. I would be a father and Michelle would be a mother. That night we called our parents, who rejoiced with us,

Now Michelle's motherly instincts kicked in. We painted the living room, dining room and baby room all within a couple of weeks. Pink and yellow abounded everywhere in our daughter's new little space. She was due in a matter of weeks, so baby showers shortly followed, five in all. Some had to wait until after she was born. We were overwhelmed with the generosity of our family, friends, and church family.

After hearing the wonderful news, I began to reflect on God's promise. First, He had given me a wife whom I loved very much. We had a great marriage. Now He had worked miraculously to give us a daughter.

Tears flowed freely down my face that evening as the magnitude of what had just happened began to grip my heart. God had been faithful.

Conclusion

The day in 2009 we called about adopting a child with Down syndrome was May 26. The day we received her as our daughter was July 17—only seven weeks. Michelle's assurance that we would have a child by Christmas had come to pass, with plenty of time to spare. On December 10, we became a family in the eyes of the court. God had worked a miracle.

Five

Y ou may be like me, and have read the story of Abraham and Sarah with bewilderment. How could these two pillars of faith doubt God's promise that they would be parents?

Years before, God had spoken directly to Abraham and revealed that he and Sarah would have a son. Yet they both laughed when they heard the news. It is easy to see why—Sarah was well past the childbearing years. God's response to them, however, was priceless: "Is anything too hard for the LORD? At the appointed time I will return to you, about this time next year, and Sarah shall have a son" (Gen. 18:14). God always comes through on His promises.

Michelle and I were a lot like Abraham and Sarah. We doubted the promise that one day we would not be childless. Before we adopted Faith, He tested us one last time through a crisis, which forced us to respond to the same question the Lord asked Abraham and Sarah: "Is anything too hard for God?"

A Crisis of Faith

As the big day of Faith's birth approached, Michelle and I were cleared to talk with the doctors to find out Faith's medical status. When we arrived, we assumed that the doctors would go over all the possible health scenarios associated with Down syndrome. They did this, and much more. The doctors also informed us that there was a good chance that Faith might have something we never considered called Dandy Walker syndrome. If this was correct, Faith might have a brain malformation centered in the cerebellum, the portion of the brain at the back of the skull that contributes to motor control and coordination. It meant she would likely not be able to walk, talk, or even feed herself. She might even have a shortened life span—or even die before we got to know her.

Michelle and I were devastated. Michelle sobbed uncontrollably on the way home. When we finally arrived at the house, I sat down in front of my computer, feverishly researching everything I could find about this syndrome. Michelle, on the other hand, went into the baby's room, prostrated herself, with her face to the floor, and began to cry out to God. A little while later, she called one of her friends to come over to console her and pray with her.

While Michelle was waiting for her friend, I called my mom. When she answered the phone, I told her the diagnosis. Her answer hit home. She told me that when I was younger, during one of my stays at Riley Hospital, she remembered a woman who gave birth to a severely deformed young girl. That girl's mother had said, "I can't raise someone like that." She left and never came back. As soon as my mom told me the story, I knew that I couldn't be that type of parent. God had made it clear to me that Faith was our daughter, and no disease was going to change that fact. Even if it meant raising a daughter with this degree of disability, we would do it.

A little later, Michelle's friend arrived. They immediately went to Faith's crib and started to pray. Up to this point, Michelle hadn't been able to form words for prayer. Instead, she spent her time crying out to God in tears. Her friend prayed that Faith was created in the image of God and that He had her in the palm of His hand. Nothing could touch her without His say so. Finally, Michelle could utter words in prayer and felt almost a literal burden lift from her shoulders. She knew in that moment that either Faith would be completely fine or God would provide a means of handling any problems that Faith might have. We are so thankful that we made the commitment to our daughter and refused to back out.

Faith Is Born

On July 17, 2009, just a few days later after the fateful doctor's visit, we received the call that Faith was born in Fort Wayne. The birth father told Michelle that the hospital there would transfer Faith to us once she and the birth mother were stabilized. We were overjoyed.

We still weren't sure what was ahead regarding Faith's health, but we knew that God was in control. On the way to the hospital in Indianapolis, which was about 90 minutes away, Michelle and I discussed the many possible health scenarios. But whatever they turned out to be, she was our daughter now. We could hardly contain our excitement.

Finally, Faith arrived at the hospital in Indianapolis. Both delighted and very concerned, we wondered: Did she have Dandy Walker syndrome? Would she ever walk or talk? Would we have to bathe her and feed her for the rest of her life because she would not be able to do it for herself?

The medical staff brought her to the Neonatal [Intensive?] Care (NIC) unit. The room included several baby beds, sectioned off by small walls that created small areas for families to visit their babies.

Then we saw her. It seemed like the pressures of the world melted away as we instantly fell in love with our precious daughter. One thing we noticed was that Faith's arms and legs were quite active—a good sign, we thought.

A few doctors came by to check on her within the first couple hours. But the doctor we wanted to see was the neurologist. When he started to check on Faith, we immediately sought his opinion. The neurologist instructed an ultrasound technician to show him Faith's brain, saying, "We need to diagnose Faith immediately, so we can put her parents' minds to rest." The technician would need an order to do that. The neurologist immediately walked around the corner, wrote one, and handed it over.

The technician then performed the test in front of us and said, with a twinkle in his eye, "Your daughter is fine. I see a fully developed cerebellum and no water on the brain." Michelle responded with tears of joy flowing down her face. We both had an incredible sense of the faithfulness of God and could now fully enjoy the arrival of our beautiful baby girl.

That is how our hospital journey began. Though the diagnosis we feared had not come, Faith still had health issues. We knew before that she would be born with duodenal atresia, an intestinal obstruction that is easily cured with surgery, but fatal if left unattended. The hospital stay Faith endured was not a shock, but it was still very trying in many ways. Her healing would require a full two months.

During this time, I played the same role that my mother played when I was a child. I had around 20 surgeries at Riley Hospital for the first several years of my life. My mom stayed at the hospital, sleeping on couches and eating out of the canteen as I recovered from surgery. Sometimes the recovery period would take one or two weeks. Nonetheless, she was there. Michelle and I were now the ones sleeping on the couches and eating the tasty microwavable sandwiches, complete with processed meat and cheese as my mom had done.

Faith stayed in the NIC unit the whole time. Most of the babies were premature, weighing just a few pounds. Faith, on the other hand, weighed over eight pounds at birth. I often joked that if the hospital put together a basketball team, Faith would play center.

While we were there, we saw so many babies come and go. Some stayed for a day or two. Others stayed for weeks or even months. Whenever a baby went home, there was joy for that family, but also a sense of sadness for us as we wondered when our turn would come.

There were also heartbreaking moments. At least three babies died. Each time, some members of the staff sang a respectful song and then ceremoniously wrapped the infant and then took him or her out the front door. One evening a baby passed away just a few beds from where Faith was sleeping. I heard the parents lamenting the loss of their little one. While I was listening, I looked down at Faith, realizing the precious gift I had been given. I thought how hard it would be to endure such a loss. My heart went out to that family. Now that we had a baby of our own, tragedies such as that one took on a whole new meaning for me.

Visiting Our Precious Gift

Several friends and family members paid visits. My best friend, Jeff, his wife, Melissa, and their daughter, Ariel, were the first. He and I, together with our wives, served together at the church in Terre Haute several years earlier. They were like family to me. Michelle and I were there when Ariel was born. Through the years I watched Jeff and Melissa raise their daughter into a beautiful young girl. Now, nearly 19 years later, it was my turn to raise a daughter.

My grandmother and my mom were the first to go in from among my family members. This moment was particularly special for my grandmother, who was in her late 80s. She was convinced that this might be her last grandchild. She didn't know that my little brother would also have a child a few years later for her to enjoy as well.

My grandmother couldn't help but voice her excitement as she approached the baby. She never thought this day would come—but it had. As soon as she sat down beside Faith's bed, the nurse gently gathered Faith out of her crib and nestled her on my grandmother's lap. My grandmother was smitten. She said, "This is the cutest baby I have ever seen." I was pleased by her comment and disappointed at the same time, knowing that I was now demoted to second place.

My mother had a similar reaction. She told me that when she had me she felt impressed that I was special, set apart for a specific purpose. While I don't feel that special calling personally, I agree with her thoughts regarding Faith. We all felt that Faith was not only our special gift from God, but that she was going to impact many lives for God's glory.

29

Why God chose us to be her parents will be the first question I ask God when I get to heaven. Until then, I will joyfully serve in my role as her father and give her all the love, attention, and training I can so she can fulfill God's calling for her life.

Born to Be a Mom

As friend after friend and relative after relative stopped by, everyone echoed the same statement—Faith was special. While this was nice to hear, what I found particularly rewarding was how Michelle instantaneously took to motherhood. It did not surprise me, since I had watched her selflessly love and care for countless kids over the years as we ministered in various social settings. Even so, it brought me great joy and satisfaction to see her fulfill a calling God had placed on her life: motherhood.

As a former pastor, I had preached sermons on motherhood and was acquainted with the various scriptures that spoke of this calling. Now I could see it modeled right before my eyes. Michelle sacrificed as she sat by Faith's bed, grabbing an hour of sleep here and there during the night for the first few days. It was evident she was the nurturing mother who would be quick to get up in the middle of the night when her daughter was sick and listen for every sniffle and know just what her child needed.

I also knew of her sincere faith in Christ, which I was fortunate to witness. I also knew that it would be transferred to Faith as Michelle sought to mold her daughter into the person God created her to be. These characteristics and many more that Michelle exemplified can be summed up in Proverbs 31, in which Solomon revealed the ideal wife and mother.

Discovering Fatherhood in the Hospital

Over the years, I often wondered what fatherhood would feel like, particularly around Father's Day, when other fathers were celebrating this day with their children. I didn't have a child or a father with which to celebrate. Now things had changed. Faith was my new reason to celebrate.

On the first night, as she slept in her hospital bed, I experienced an incredible sense of gratitude toward God. I was now a father, which felt both great and humbling. I had studied the concept of fatherhood in the Bible many times. For years, I sought to draw truths from Scripture to equip men to be good fathers to their children. Suddenly, with Faith, I knew I had to apply those truths to my own life.

I knew that I was called to walk in integrity so I could be a model for Faith (Prov. 20:7). I was not to provoke my child to anger, but teach her the things of God (Eph. 6:4). I was to show compassion to her (Psalm 103:13) and discipline her when necessary (Prov. 13:24). She would be the primary person I was to disciple. My spiritual maturity would now grow in new ways because of my daughter.

Faith is My New Ministry

I served for several years in ministry before Faith became part of our family. I had spent countless hours counseling, equipping, building relationships, and sharing the gospel as a pastor. Much of my time was spent ministering to broken hearts and lives.

Suddenly, my calling had changed. I set aside my personal aspirations to pastoral ministry, because my daughter, Faith, had become my new ministry. This ministry began in the hospital the first day I saw her and sprang from my profound gratitude to God. I had done nothing to deserve this gift.

Years before, I had been a 21-year-old alcoholic contemplating suicide daily, finding it tough just to function without a drink. Now, despite my rebellion, my hatred, and my hard heart toward God, He reached down and drew me to Himself. He replaced a heart of stone with one that had been impacted by God's love and grace. Now, with a heart full of gratitude, I was a father to Faith.

The gospel changes a person. While I always knew this truth, it was taking on a new meaning in my life. Having done a significant work in my heart to prepare me to be a father, the illuminating ministry of the Holy Spirit was continuing to reveal the truth about the riches I already had in the gospel. The Bible made clear that before I was a Christian, I was an unworthy sinner in need of redemption. There was nothing I could have done to save myself. No good work would be enough. No penance would suffice. No human could intercede on my behalf. But Jesus paid the price for my sins by serving as a substitute, taking the penalty of my sin upon Himself. He then saved me by drawing me to Himself. No work on my part was necessary. I simply accepted the gift. Now, more than ever, the Holy Spirit was crystallizing these truths to me. I knew I was deeply loved and fully pleasing to God.

I had an overwhelming sense of how much the hand of God was orchestrating these events. God loved Michelle and me, and He was bestowing on us an incredible gift. The events that led to Faith entering our lives made it abundantly clear how much God loved us and how blessed we were. He had heard our many prayers—the prayers of a woman who could not have children as well as the prayers of a man who hated Father's Day because he had no child with whom to celebrate it. As with Hannah of old, God worked out a miracle and brought us a child.

The Hospital Stay

The two months in the hospital with Faith were grueling for Michelle and me. After the first week, daily we drove back and forth 90 minutes each way to spend time with her. We brought our work with us and either did it on the way or while we were by her side.

Our dinners on the way were fast food—except on Fridays when we would stay the weekend. The hospital had a special plan for families with extended stays. Families could stay at the hotel on campus two days every week. On weekends, then, we lived out of a suitcase. We were educators, not business people, so this was new to us. Yet we adapted rather easily, grateful for the hospital's provision.

During this time, we had much to learn before taking our baby home. During the first week, the nurse gave me a tutorial on changing a diaper. I figured that Michelle, who already knew how to change diapers, was prequalified for this duty. As the nurse was training me, I felt it was just a waste of time. I discovered later how wrong I was when we brought Faith home!

Feeding became one of Faith's major issues. She had to have an NG tube most of the time. Also known as a nasogastric tube, it is inserted through the nose, past the throat and down to the stomach so children receive can receive the essential calories and nutrients they would receive during normal eating.

Because of the NG tube, it was very difficult for Faith to learn to take the bottle on her own. She never did learn to take the bottle while in the hospital, so it was necessary to put in a G tube, known as a gastronomy tube. This one is inserted surgically and goes directly to the stomach. The nurses trained us on how to feed her this way, our last hurdle before leaving the hospital and taking our baby home. This task was scary at first, since we had never done anything like it before. But once we had learned the feeding procedures Faith was ready to go home!

On that day, we were overjoyed. Packing her things into the car, we thanked the nurses for all their love and support and bid them farewell. We were amazed at how many gifts for Faith that we had accumulated. It was time to take Faith home on her very first car ride. She was about to embark on a new journey, life outside the hospital.

Conclusion

For the next six years, Michelle and I raised Faith, growing together as a family. Michelle and Faith developed a very close mother/daughter relationship. Michelle developed fun routines with Faith that cemented her relationship—cleaning up the room, bathing, and brushing teeth, for example.

However, perhaps the greatest bonding device that Michelle utilized was simply giving her time. She invested countless hours helping with homework, playing board games, and just hanging out. But one day we received news from the doctor that eventually would change the mother daughter relationship forever.

Six

Bad News

For nearly six years, I lived my personal American Dream. I was married to the woman I loved and had grown deeper in my love for her as we shared life. The promise of a child had also been fulfilled. Faith was in the second semester of her kindergarten year and had come so far in her growth. She was thriving.

Then one morning before work, as I was fixing the family breakfast, something happened to Michelle. As I was frying eggs, Michelle was making her way behind me to the other side of the kitchen. Suddenly, she doubled over, complaining of a shooting pain in her rib area.

To gather herself and figure out what was happening, she sat in the chair near the kitchen table. I immediately offered to call the doctor. However, she wanted to wait and see if the pain continued. After a few minutes, it subsided, so she ate breakfast and finished getting ready for work.

That evening, we all sat down for dinner. It was our custom to allow each family member to share about the day. Faith began by telling us what she did at recess, which was her favorite subject that year. I followed by telling about the mundane day I had endured. Regrettably, I had forgotten about what had happened to Michelle earlier that morning.

After I finished, Michelle chimed in. She reminded us about the painful episode that morning but said she had been fine the rest of the day. There were no hints of any pain all day. We both concluded that there was nothing to worry about, unless the pain reemerged. For the next few days, there was no pain, so we assumed everything was fine.

About a week after the first muscle spasm, however, Michelle experienced another one, except this time much worse. As she was walking into the kitchen, she suddenly felt a riveting pain shoot through her back. Then Michelle's knees buckled and hobbled to the chaise lounge chair. With intense pain displayed on her face, she began crying and screaming. We were all bewildered and frightened.

Later that week, a few hours after Michelle had gone to bed, she felt excruciating pain through her back, centered in her rib area. She woke up screaming. I was deeply asleep beside her, dreaming. Michelle struck me on the hip to wake me up. When I asked her what was the matter, she said through her tears that something bad had happened. I grabbed my cell phone and dialed 911.

When the ambulance arrived, Michelle was still crying out in pain in the living room. Faith woke up, wanting to know what was going on. I told her that Mommy was in some pain and the people in the living room helping her were going to take her to the doctor so she could feel better again. Fortunately, in Faith's eyes, doctors always make things better. This put her mind at ease. I promised her that everything was going to be okay and instructed her to go back to bed. Since she was still very tired, she responded without any resistance and laid down again and fell asleep.

After the ambulance left, I went to the bedroom to awaken Faith and help her get dressed. We were going to the hospital, too.

On our way, Faith sat quietly in her car seat. When I looked at my daughter through the rearview mirror, she appeared worried. After a few minutes, she asked if Mommy was going to be okay. I told her she was going to be fine, but I wondered what was going on. Still, I never imagined how bad the news would be.

When we arrived at the hospital, the nurse told me that the doctor had ordered X-rays. and escorted Faith and me to Michelle's room. Michelle was still in pain, and I felt helpless, wanting to make it better. A few minutes later, another nurse escorted Michelle to get the X-rays. After about 30 minutes, Michelle returned, feeling better. The pain medicine had apparently started to work.

An hour later, when the X-ray results came in, the doctor said that Michelle had fractured one of her ribs due to muscle spasms. He also read her medical history and saw she had osteopenia and hypothesized that the fracture might be due to her moving from osteopenia to osteoporosis.

Michelle was told to follow up with her family doctor. He too thought that she probably just had osteoporosis but wanted to follow up with a nuclear bone scan just in case. A few days later, the bone density test results were in. The results pointed to cancer.

Later that day, I called my friend Mike with the news. He wisely suggested getting a second or even a third opinion. Fortunately, Mike knew some very respected oncologists and had Michelle's X-rays sent to them.

Given her condition, Michelle did not to go to work for the next few weeks. She couldn't do much around the house and wanted the comfort that only a mother can provide. Her mom was at our home the very next day.

When Sunday rolled around, Faith and I went to church while Michelle's mom stayed with her. I forced myself to go, knowing I needed to. Two of my friends greeted me at the door, asking how I was doing. I told them I was fine and kept walking. If I told them how I really felt, I was afraid I would start crying uncontrollably, as I had yet to begin processing what I was feeling. I wanted to be strong for Michelle and Faith.

After dropping Faith off at the kids' class, I went to the sanctuary. It was about 15 minutes before the service was to begin. Not many people were there, which was fine with me. I just wanted sit alone and think, but the sick feeling in my stomach made it nearly impossible to experience a sustained thought. A couple minutes later, someone sat down and talked to me until the service started. I was grateful for his kind words.

After church, Faith and I met Mike and his family for lunch at a Mexican restaurant. I braced myself because it was apparent that he was hesitant to share the news from his doctor friends. He told me that Michelle's condition appeared to be very serious. I couldn't believe my ears, pressing him about what they had said. He replied that the X-rays "blew up," revealing several problem areas that were probably cancer, but further tests were needed to confirm.

I was stunned. I might lose my wife, and my daughter might lose her mom.

When we arrived home an hour later, I told Michelle we needed to talk. She hobbled back to her bedroom, with me assisting. I wanted to make sure she didn't fall. When we entered, I shut the door and suggested she sit down. She discerned that the news wasn't going to be good given the tears that were already streaming down my face. She also began to cry. Hugging her, I relayed Mike's information. Putting her face in her hands, my wife sobbed almost uncontrollably, saying, "No, no, no." I was sobbing as well, telling Michelle that I didn't want to lose her.

We sat on the bed for several minutes, clutching one another tightly. It is difficult to put into words the maudlin emotions I was feeling. I wanted to fix the situation, but I felt so helpless.

On the way to Michelle's oncologist to discuss the results, I drove. We talked about what we might hear, and Michelle had bravely recovered from her earlier panic. Knowing the possibilities, she was willing to accept whatever her future held, displaying her great confidence in God.

We were immediately brought back to the examination room. Nervous and a bit perplexed, we sat there waiting for about 20 minutes. Not many words were said. We just held hands and kept our thoughts to ourselves.

When the doctor finally knocked on the door, we knew we would soon would learn Michelle's fate. While there were more tests needed to confirm the diagnosis, the doctor was sure it was cancer. Tears flowed. The future was no longer in our hands. Once again, we turned to the One who controls of all of life.

Other tests were ordered. They brought more bad news. A nuclear bone scan showed an abnormality on Michelle's skull the size of a quarter. Then came a CT scan, followed by a PET scan.

Nightly Conversations

During this ordeal, nearly every night Michelle and I stayed up until the wee hours, long after Faith and my mother-in-law went to bed. During these late-night conversations, the lights were off, with only a small candle providing the visibility we needed to see one another. We kept focusing on what would happen if Michelle didn't make it. What would life be like if she passed away? How would I deal with Faith? What about our finances? Should I remarry? These were hard but necessary questions.

Michelle was such a hard-working, energetic wife and mother. Now she began to wonder who was going to do those things if she were gone. Faith would have no mother to teach her how to be a woman. Michelle realized that she might not see Faith grow up, graduate from high school, or walk down the aisle to marry the man of her dreams. Faith's future weighed heavily on her heart.

One night, Michelle wanted to talk about *my* future if she died. At first, I balked, but Michelle persisted. I saw her compassion for me. I know it was hard for her talk about my marrying someone else. It was certainly hard for *me* to hear. Michelle didn't want me or Faith to be alone.

In hindsight, though, I am glad she pressed the issue. She felt strongly I should remarry. She knew my commitment to her. She also knew, because of that commitment, how hard it would be for me to marry someone else if she died. That night, my wife assured me that I had her blessing, if the situation presented itself.

Things that Brought Comfort

All the while, Michelle suffered terribly. The slightest move the wrong way made her scream in pain. It was hard for the family to watch. We couldn't help but fear that she might be dying right before our eyes.

Two things brought Michelle relief and comfort. The first was worship music. A member of the high school band who later majored in flute in her first year of college, Michelle was also asked to be on the worship team with a small campus group at her college. So I wasn't surprised when she turned to worship music to help her get through the pain. She was treating God as if he were God. He was worthy of worship because of who He was and not for what He did for her. Her situation was under His control, and she was determined to praise Him.

For Michelle, worship was a way of life. She enjoyed worshiping God because He is worthy of worship. He was her source of peace; worshiping God was where she found rest. She followed the advice of Elisabeth Elliot, who said, "God is God. If He is God, He is worthy of my worship and my service. I will find rest nowhere but in His will, and that will infinitely, immeasurably, unspeakably beyond my largest notions of what He is up to."[15] This trial revealed the source of her strength. Suffering often reveals where we are placing our trust.

There were two worship songs she listened to over and over. One was by Chris Tomlin titled *Good, Good, Father*. I bet we listened to this song together at least five times a day. The words were like a healing balm for Michelle. The song includes the following words.

Oh, I've heard a thousand stories of what they think you're like
But I've heard the tender whispers of love in the dead of night
And you tell me that you're pleased
And that I'm never alone

You're a Good, Good Father

---

15 Quoted in Keller, Kindle Locations 4505-4507.

There are different ways Michelle could have reacted to her suffering. She could have gotten angry at God. Adversity tempts us to stop seeing God as our loving Heavenly Father. We doubt His love and even begin to see Him as sinister and as someone who is indifferent to or perhaps who even delights in our pain. If it is not dealt with, this kind of anger can easily turn into hatred toward God.

Or Michelle could have responded with spiritual withdrawal. When suffering occurs, some people don't deny God. They simply distance themselves from Him. They stop reading their Bibles, praying, or attending church. Often, these individuals suppress their feelings.

The response Michelle chose, however, was to acknowledge God as a loving Heavenly Father and express her love for Him. God created men and women to have a relationship with him. Michelle chose this option because she understood this and sought to relate with God during her trial. During her suffering, she acknowledged God and related to Him as her Heavenly Father. She wanted to express her love and devotion to Him.

The words in the song reminded Michelle that God was a good Father who would never leave her nor forsake her. She needed this ongoing reminder that God was pleased with and loved her. He has created us as relational beings, so he can fill our heart's longing for a loving relationship with Him. Often our times of struggle make us most conscious of our need for Him, which was the case for Michelle.

Another song that ministered to her was *Deliverer*, by Matt Maher. Michelle needed to be reminded that God was her deliverer, despite not knowing what her future held.

The Apostle Paul also saw God as his deliverer, either in this life or the next, which is why he said, "For me to live is Christ and to die is gain" (Phil. 1:21). He knew the ministry he could do if he remained on earth and the lives he would impact. Yet, if Paul were to die, he was assured of eternal life. Therefore, he said, "If I am to live in the flesh, that means fruitful labor for me. Yet which I shall choose I cannot tell. I am hard pressed between the two. My desire is to depart and be with Christ, for that is far better" (Phil. 1:22-23). Either way, God was his deliverer.

Michelle understood this. God would either heal her or she would receive her eternal reward in heaven. Either way, she was a winner because God was her deliverer.

The second source of Michelle's comfort were Faith's prayers. It wasn't uncommon to see Faith walk over to her mom and lay hands on her to pray when Michelle was hurting. This was something Faith had been taught over the years.

Prayer was something Faith had been taught her entire life. She learned the importance of prayer at the dinner table, as did I. When I was a boy, my family came together for dinner to eat and talk about what happened during our day. It was a sacred time that didn't allow for disruptions like a television show or a sporting event. We all had to be at the dinner table ready to eat at 6 p.m.

When we adopted Faith, we decided to sit together at the table for supper. One of our goals was to pray together before eating. We did this with Faith from the beginning, even before she understood the meaning of prayer. When she was old enough, she folded her hands to pray, but she didn't say anything; normally, she would look down and smile, knowing we were focused on her and were inviting her to participate. Sometime around the age of 4 or 5, that began to change. I usually prayed for the meal, but now Faith asked to pray, too. She would say, "Faith pray," and would bow her head, exhort everyone else at the table to hold hands and bow their heads, and then begin to mouth some words. After about 30 seconds, she would say an enthusiastic "Amen" for a finale. She learned through observation and much repetition that we were to pray for our food and give thanks.

While these dinner prayers had value, the broader goal was to teach Faith to pray. Before Faith went to bed, we also prayed together. Before a trip, we prayed for safety. When she was struggling at school, we prayed together about it. When Faith was sick, Michelle and I laid hands on her and prayed for her. So it was no surprise to see Faith laying hands on her mom and praying for her without being asked. What a blessing for Michelle!

The Power of Prayer

Michelle and I really valued prayer for ourselves, which is why we enlisted as many people as we could to pray with us for her healing. We had seen tremendous results over the years and were confident that God could bring Michelle back to normal health.

Our church continued to pray fervently for Michelle. I asked church members to pray that God would grant the doctors wisdom, so they could treat whatever she had. I also asked for prayers for her healing, and for peace for both of us.

God sent other people to pray as well. Three ladies from Faith's school—Sydell, Theresa, and Sunny—stood with our family the entire time. They not only continued to pray for Michelle, but took our requests to their respective churches to pray as well. Their text messages of encouragement were invaluable throughout.

As people prayed, Michelle's condition seemed to improve. Test after test in the ensuing weeks revealed good news. The first two biopsies of her thyroid and lung came back normal. Then we heard that the third biopsy (bone) was also normal. Upon hearing the news, Michelle asked if cancer was still possible, and the doctor said that although she couldn't rule it out, things looked very, very good.

There were two more tests, a PET scan and more blood work. While the first revealed massive problems, the second one officially ruled out cancer!

By this time, the spasms were gone, and Michelle felt fine. Off work for about three months, she was ready to return. Even though the physicians still didn't know why the one test had turned out that way, Michelle's prognosis was no longer deemed possibly terminal.

Michelle's students were thrilled to have her back. They loved her because of the way she poured herself into their lives. Her fellow teachers, with whom she had a close bond, were also glad to see her.

Everything seemed to be back to normal. Our oncologist did, however, mention a few possibilities, but all were treatable.

Michelle felt good physically. It was obvious to us and everyone else, our prayers were answered. The scare that we received was not to be. Michelle would be involved in Faith's life for many years to come. It is difficult to put into words our joy and relief.

Others phoned us and sent emails sharing in our excitement. For example, I received the following note from my good friend, Harold. He rejoiced with us, as he shared the news with his friends the results of their prayers.

"THEY HAVE FOUND NO CANCER!!!"

I received this text earlier from Tim Orr. A few weeks ago, I sent you an email describing the devastating news this couple had just received that Michelle had cancer. Michelle had broken a rib through the simple act of coughing. Further diagnosis determined bone cancer was the likely culprit. When doctors performed a PET scan her results lit up so dramatically throughout her body that doctors immediately began preparing the family for the worst. When shown the tests, other doctors in the area confirmed the initial diagnosis.

The Orr's are close friends, have dedicated their lives to serving the Lord in ministry, and when they were unable to conceive a child they choose to adopt; specifically seeking a child with special needs (Down syndrome) to become their daughter. What is further remarkable about this couple are the trials Tim experienced growing up with his own severe health issues, battle with alcoholism and feelings of rejection. I won't spend further time here, but Tim has written a book that is available on Amazon entitled "We Named her Faith" describing his experiences in greater detail and how it has shaped his faith.

For the past few weeks hundreds of people, including some of you, have gone to God in prayer asking God to heal Michelle. Considering the severity of the initial diagnosis, we have been praying for nothing short of a miracle. Slowly, over the past few weeks, doctors have tried to isolate and identify the severity of the cancer. The idea that the cancer might have originated in Michelle's lungs and spread to her bones was disproven. Tests to find cancer in her bones and other areas of her body were also negative. Finally, the doctors decided to perform another PET scan. The results of this second test are relayed to you at the beginning of this email.

I have had to deal with my own doubts and frustrations before God concerning Michelle's health. Why would God allow a couple who has already been through so much and has dedicated their lives to serving God by being His expression of Love to others be put into this terrible position? If Tim and Faith lost Michelle, what would happen to them? I know God is Sovereign and Romans 8:28 says that "in all things God works for the good of those who love Him, and have been called according to His purpose." but this situation seemed especially harsh. I know with certainty that had the tests come back less favorable the Orr's would have continued to place their trust in Him and God would have still been glorified. But today we to celebrate a miracle of healing. What a Mighty God we serve!

Harold

Harold's letter captured our thoughts nicely. We were overjoyed. I wasn't going to lose my wife and Faith was not going to lose her mother! It turns out that we had just experienced a minor setback.

Seven

You probably remember, as I do, studying government in school. We had to grasp the divisions of power, memorize the names of all the presidents, and learn the Declaration of Independence, which says that people are endowed with certain rights given by God, including "life, liberty, and the pursuit of happiness." Thus, we understood the American Dream to mean that people who worked hard could advance in life and prosper according to their abilities. This ethos was taught in school, and I believed it.

American Dream

After my conversion, I still believed in the American Dream. My own pursuit of happiness consisted of having a wife, 2.5 kids, and the house with the white picket fence that this dream promised. By God's grace, I realized the first part of that dream 23 years earlier when I married Michelle. Then came the house with the white picket fence. It took 16 years after we were married until I inherited the final part of the promise, with a child joining our family. I was now fully living my American Dream.

When we received the news about Michelle's cancer, however, this dream was shattered. But the scare was short-lived, as we learned that

Michelle didn't have cancer after all. The threat of losing the life I thought I was entitled to was gone. Consequently, we wanted to celebrate, but how?

Reminiscing about Disney

I made my first trip to Walt Disney World when I was a boy. My family didn't have the money to make such a trip, but I was able to go with my cousin Jeff and his family. I looked forward to the trip for weeks. My excitement grew when Jeff's mom and dad told me about the attractions I would enjoy when I got there.

Jeff had already been there several times, as Disney served as the yearly vacation spot for his family. A couple weeks before the trip, we were talking and his face beamed with excitement as he began to describe the fun we would have riding Space Mountain, Big Thunder Mountain Railroad, and the Haunted Mansion. The Polynesian Resort Hotel, where we would stay, had a pool where we would swim nightly after enjoying the entire day at the park.

And the experience did not disappoint. When the trip was over, I was sold on the "magic kingdom." For me, it was the happiest place on earth. My wife also traveled to Disney when she was a child and enjoyed a similar experience.

So I wanted my daughter to have that same experience. Since we adopted Faith, this was on our list of things to do when she was old enough. Now that she was almost 6, we concluded it was time. Finding out that Michelle didn't have cancer presented our family with the perfect opportunity.

Off to Disney

For two months, Michelle worked diligently with our friend Zoe to plan the trip. They wanted everything to be perfect. At one point in the process, Zoe commented to Michelle, "We've been praying for you guys. I hope Disney World can give you a little break from the brokenness of the real world and that you make lots of new memories together."

As the trip drew closer, the excitement began to build. One evening, as we were driving to a restaurant for dinner, we shared our nearly forgotten memories about Disney. It was like opening a scrapbook from decades before.

During my first trip to Disney, I rode The Pirates of the Caribbean. We boarded the small craft, allowing us to experience the Disney version of a high-seas adventure. The part of that ride that filled my mind simultaneously with both terror and excitement was the small waterfall that catapulted us down a 10-foot drop. As an adult, I find the drop quite unimpressive, but as a child, it was a fun-filled adventure.

To capture these experiences as a family, we made sure that we had pictures, so the memories could be relived repeatedly. We decided to get a Disney World photo pass so Michelle and I could enjoy the full experience when Faith was meeting the Disney characters behind the scenes.

The Dining Experience

Our trip turned out to be wonderful, and much of our pleasure came from watching Faith's reactions to attractions such as the Mad Tea Party or Peter Pan's Flight, not to mention the Country Bear Jamboree.

A Disney experience would not be complete without a few dining experiences that put the finishing touches on an evening. One of our favorite restaurants there is called Boma, an all- you-can-eat buffet featuring dishes from a variety of African countries. Faith was captivated by the artwork, as well as the seemingly mile-long buffet. She asked about some of the food, but even I had no idea what some of the choices were.

Once in the line, Faith seemingly wanted us to put each item on her plate. As her parents, however, we knew what items she would and wouldn't like and proceeded accordingly.

Over a great meal together, we discussed our day and found out what parts of the Disney experience Faith enjoyed the most. Bursting with excitement, as she told us how much she liked meeting Mickey Mouse and getting his autograph. Her summary of her favorite rides was quite entertaining.

This experience was everything Michelle and I wanted it to be. The six years we waited to take Faith were all worth it. There is nothing like watching the joy on the face of a child who has just fallen in love with Disney World for the first time.

Going Back Home

At the time, I hadn't yet overcome my fear of flying. On our flight home, I boarded the plane with a troubled look on my face. Equally troubled was Faith, who hadn't overcome her fear of flying, either. Fortunately, a flight attendant named Barb engaged us in conversation to calm our nerves. When Barb asked about our trip, it was our delight to tell her the backstory of what had happened and our need to celebrate our good news at Disney.

Conclusion

During this trip, we all grew closer. We were so grateful that Faith could experience Disney World. With joy she rode the Dumbo ride, the Mad Tea Party, and Peter Pan's Flight. In her book, *City of Heavenly Fire*, Cassandra Clare says, "There are memories that time does not erase."[16] I hope that these memories will last forever for Faith.

I picture her sitting around the lunch table at school telling another student about her experience. As she shares, I want my daughter to realize the bonds that were made between her, Michelle, and me.

---

16 Cassandra Clare, *City of Heavenly Fire (The Mortal Instruments, Book 6)* (New York: Margaret K. McElderry Books, 2014), 231.

Eight

MICHELLE PASSES AWAY

For several years, Michelle had worked during summer schools. This sacrifice on her part gave us the money to take our yearly vacations. However, in 2016 we waited patiently to see if Michelle's school district wanted to hire her again. She usually received word by April, but this time it was almost summer break, and we had not heard. Michelle finally decided that, because of all that had gone on during the regular school year, she would simply enjoy her summer break. In hindsight, I am glad she did.

With her cancer-free diagnosis, we had plenty to celebrate. The past few months had been an emotional rollercoaster. Though the doctors still hadn't settled on a diagnosis, her formerly bleak outlook was gone. Though there might be medical issues ahead, we assumed the family would still be intact.

By the first week of June, we had already finished our summer vacation. But Michelle still had plenty of plans to take Faith to the park, play games with her, and just celebrate the fact that she would be around for a long time.

Every summer, Michelle took at least two trips to go to Michigan to see her family, and this year would be no exception. The night before she left for her June trip, Michelle packed and got ready for the six-hour drive. She had a routine of washing every piece of clothing in the house. I am not sure why, but I was always thankful for the two-week supply of clean clothes.

After she finished packing, Michelle sat by me on the couch. I just held her for a few minutes, grateful to have my healthy wife beside me. Things had been tough the past six months. Many nights I had stayed awake long after everyone went to bed, wondering about our future. My mind had been bombarded with questions. How would I help Faith walk through the loss if Michelle were to die? Would Faith be severely affected? Would I? As I held Michelle in my arms now, I was sure that those questions no longer needed to be asked.

The next day, I fixed breakfast for Michelle and Faith, who were plenty excited about the trip. Michelle had been explaining to Faith all the good times they were going to enjoy. Faith couldn't wait to get to Michigan, so she could see the horses and take in the beautiful Michigan scenery. Together we packed up the car, and the two of them were ready to go.

Our tradition as a couple was to kiss each other before either one of us left. Since our first year of marriage, she would ask me to give her a kiss, followed by her routine statement, "You never know if this will be the last time we will see one another." When she left this time, she again uttered those familiar words.

After I kissed them both goodbye, Michelle and Faith took off while I stayed home to work. As usual, Michelle called me at the halfway point and then again when she arrived. I heard the excitement in her voice. She loved her family and worked hard to include Faith.

A few days later, Michelle wasn't feeling very well but decided to take Faith to the park anyway. There was nothing Faith loved to do more than spend that quality time with Mom, having fun on the swings and the slide.

When Michelle and Faith left the park, they stopped by her mom's house, where they were staying. They visited for a short time, then left for her sister's place, about 30 minutes away.

Approximately an hour after they left, I received a phone call from Michelle's mother. She wanted to know if I had heard from her. She had not yet arrived at her sister's. Many times during our marriage Michelle would stop and get something to eat or drink without telling anyone, then be on her way. I assumed that this was one of those times.

After I told Michelle's mom I would call her back if I heard from her, she hung up and called the police. They informed her that both Michelle and Faith had been in a bad accident and were being rushed to the hospital. Immediately she called me. As soon as I heard the news, I feverishly began to text anyone I could to have them pray.

A few minutes later, when Michelle's mother arrived at the scene, she discovered that it wasn't a wreck and that Faith was fine. Michelle had pulled off to the side of the road and lost consciousness. After a few minutes, Faith, who was in the back seat, got out of her seat and tried, as she later said, "to wake Mommy up." Luckily, a passer-by saw what happened, pulled over, and called the ambulance.

Michelle's mom called me again, and I asked to talk to the officer on duty. When I pressed him about Michelle's condition when she was taken to the hospital, his reply shocked me. She was unconscious, and the paramedics were trying to revive her.

About 20 minutes later, my mother-in-law called again. "I don't know how to tell you this," she said. I swallowed hard and braced myself. Then I heard the words, "Michelle's gone." She had died with Faith on her lap.

I hung up, dropped to my knees, and kept screaming, "No, no, no!" The wife I loved so much was dead. After three months of agony wondering if Michelle was dying of cancer followed by a cancer-free diagnosis, now I received *this* news? It was too much to take.

Frantically, I called my pastor and told him. I kept asking him what I was going to do. I was left to raise a special needs daughter by myself. I was living a nightmare. Michelle had been given a clean bill of health. Now I asked God, "Why?"

Shortly after I heard the news, my church sent out this email:

Dear Brothers and Sisters,

It is with deep sorrow and grief that I write to inform you that our beautiful sister, Michelle, passed away just a little while ago. Tim is on his way with Danny [the senior pastor] and others to where Michelle and Faith were traveling in Michigan. Many questions are in our minds and hearts at a time like this. There is, however, one profound certainty. Jesus is with us. He was with Michelle and Faith earlier today and He is with Tim and all of us who grieve, now.

"Fear not, for I have redeemed you; I have called you by name, you are mine. When you pass through the waters, I will be with you; and through the rivers, they shall not overwhelm you; when you walk through fire you shall not be burned, and the flame shall not consume you. For I am the Lord your God, the Holy One of Israel, your Savior."

We cry out to You, Lord Jesus, in anguish for our brother, Tim, and dear precious Faith. Comfort them in their pain, help them to keep their eyes on You. There is no place else to turn except to You. Help us, Lord, too. We trust You, Jesus. We love you and we pray for Your presence and mercy and grace to be with them.

Amen

After I notified a few people that Michelle had passed away, Mike came over to take me, along with two other friends, to Michigan where Michelle passed away. It took about eight hours to get there, so I had a lot of time to think.

I was emotionally frozen. I didn't quite know what I was feeling. However, I had read enough about grieving to know that I had a long road ahead of me. What troubled me the most, though, was how Faith was going to react. Would this have permanent effects on her? The mother/daughter bond was so strong. How was this going to be replaced?

Feelings of inadequacy also began to surface. How was I going to raise a child with special needs by myself? Michelle and I had raised Faith as a team. We even did the bedtime routine together. The loss was not going to be easily replaced.

It was probably 10 p.m. when we finally arrived. Michelle's mom filled me in on further details. We were still in shock. After our conversation, I walked over to the bedroom where Faith was sleeping and quietly opened the door. She was lying there so innocently, with a slight smile. She was obviously having a pleasant dream. I laid down beside her, clutching her against me, not wanting to let her go. After about an hour, I too fell asleep.

The next day, Faith and I woke up at the same time. She reached over to give me a hug, not fully realizing what had happened. "Where is Mommy?" she asked. I told her that Mommy had gone home to be with Jesus last night. Her response almost made me burst into tears.

"Daddy," she said, "I couldn't wake Mommy up. How come I couldn't wake Mommy up?" She added that she even tried to pull Michelle's hair to awaken her, but to no avail. This would be the last memory Faith would have of her mother. I wasn't sure what to do at that point.

Later that day, we traveled to the funeral home in Michigan to plan Michelle's service. Emotionally, I was yet to come to terms with what had happened. But I gutted it out.

Since there would be two funerals, one in Michigan and a memorial back home in Indiana, I decided to let Michelle's family have the most input for this one. This would be the last time they would see Michelle, so I wanted the service to be as meaningful for them as possible.

The next day, the day before the service, the funeral home let me see Michelle. I had not seen her since the day we both said goodbye. Mike drove me there. I remember arriving, taking a deep breath, and telling Mike that I wasn't sure I could do this. He encouraged me, and I went in.

The director greeted us at the door, telling me that Michelle's body was in the next room, ready for me to view. Mike patted me on the shoulder and told me it would be a good idea for me to go in alone.

I walked in slowly, not wanting to see what I was going to see. For the entire 23 years of our marriage, I daydreamed about Michelle and me growing old, sitting on a front porch, holding hands, and just talking. I assumed that we would grow old together along with our love for one another. I never considered that my plan would be cut short.

I was quickly jolted into reality. The staff had arranged a seat for me next to the casket. I sat in it and just stared at Michelle's body for several minutes, trying to gather my thoughts, trying to process what had happened. Even though what lay before me was a corpse, I talked to Michelle as if she were still alive. Through my tears, I told her how much I loved her, how thankful I was for her, and how appreciative I was of the difference she had made in my life.

My mind returned to the times she had encouraged me, prayed for me, and even admonished me. It was as if I was not only telling her goodbye, but taking advantage of this last opportunity to thank her for the impact she had made. After I poured my heart out for several minutes and leaned over her body, I gently kissed her on the forehead and told her goodbye.

The next day, when we laid Michelle to rest, a big crowd came to say farewell to my beloved wife. Some people even traveled all the way from Columbus to pay their final respects, even though there would be a memorial service in our hometown the following week.

It was fitting that the same church that made such a dramatic influence early in her life was the church where her life was memorialized. When Michelle was 5, she attended a Sunday school class in the old building. The other children were listening intently to the lesson. When they stood to sing "Jesus Loves Me," Michelle felt God's presence fill the room. And God used this experience to impact the way Michelle felt about worship, children's ministry, and even parenting.

Michelle's Funeral

Michelle's life was truly honored at the funeral in Michigan. The pastor of her mother shared stories about Michelle, some I knew well and some I had forgotten. He described the difference her grandmother had made in her life—taking her to church, mentoring her in the early years, and continuing that relationship with Michelle until she was laid to rest. Many others testified of this godly woman's impact as well.

The service was powerful and encouraging—not just to me, but to those in attendance. Afterwards, one man told me that this was the first funeral he had ever attended where he felt better after leaving it. I believe that when Michelle was laid to rest, God decided to honor her in an incredible way.

Honor, however, is something we usually don't think God does for people. We usually see it only as our duty to honor God, which is true. But Scripture also teaches that God desires to honor his people—but how He does it differs vastly from how it is done in the world. In Matthew 20:20-28, Jesus rebukes James and John for their prideful quest to gain honor. By seeking honor in order to bolster themselves, they were following the model of the world.

Posting about the funeral a few days later, I asked if it is wrong to seek honor. I answered by explaining that it depends on one's motivation. In the passage mentioned above, Jesus was telling His disciples that if they wanted to receive honor, they must be the servant of all. Jesus, who deserves the most honor, humbled himself and did just that.

That day Michelle was honored by our Lord because she strove to be the servant of all. Many strive to receive honor by seeking the applause of men. Just get on social media for five minutes and you'll see that. As her husband of 23 years, having known her better than anyone, I can tell you that Michelle received honor that day, not because she sought the applause of other people, but because she sought the applause of God.

Memorial in Columbus

A week and a half later, we held a memorial service in Columbus, Indiana, our home for more than a decade. I wanted to give Michelle's friends, colleagues, and church family in Indiana an opportunity to say goodbye.

A few days ahead of time, I went over the service details with the church staff. I wanted Danny, the senior pastor, to give an opening statement, followed by a eulogy given by her lifelong mentor, Annette. I also suggested they play a song, titled *Good, Good Father*, that was particularly meaningful to Michelle during her cancer scare.

I would deliver the main eulogy. Years before, Michelle had asked me to do this if she passed away before I did. She requested only two things—I was to say good things about her and share the gospel. She echoed this same request during when she was going through the cancer scare five months earlier. The service would be held on Sunday afternoon, July 10.

When the day arrived, I decided that Faith and I would attend Sunday morning service at church that day. I felt we needed all the spiritual encouragement we could get. I don't remember the sermon, but I do know that it brought me the encouragement I needed.

After the church service, Faith and I, with some of our friends, went to the Mexican restaurant, our usual hangout after church. Preoccupied with my speaking responsibility at Michelle's memorial, I couldn't eat a thing. After 20 minutes, I returned to church to get ready, leaving Faith in the care of trusted friends.

As I drove, my mind was a jumbled mess. Any inner fortitude I normally had was gone. My goal was just to make it back to the church without breaking down. When I arrived, I walked to the pastor's office to gather my thoughts. For the next two hours, I prayed to God for the strength to carry out my task.

As people finally started filing into the sanctuary for the service, I tried to shake hands with each one. As they expressed their sympathies, it was clear that Michelle had touched many lives.

My prayer for strength was answered. As I sat on the platform next to Annette and Danny, I felt an incredible sense of peace and an inner boldness. When the service began, Pastor Danny slowly walked over to the podium reminded everyone the blessing that Michelle was to all of us. Annette shared a short eulogy that began with her reaction to the news that Michelle had passed away. Annette then visualized her friend worshiping Jesus in heaven, along with the angels. Michelle loved to worship.

Annette reminisced about the time when she led the singles ministries years before in Terre Haute. Michelle was one of her students. Annette recalled when Michelle asked her if she would ask her husband, Randy, to ask me if I would go on a date with her. When the question finally filtered down to me, I answered, through the same series on intermediaries, that I would love to go out with her.

Annette also told how she and Randy, my father in the faith, walked with us during the adoption process. They loved and gave us counsel the entire time. This was the fruit of a 25-year friendship. Friendships like this are not built in a day.

Annette also shared how Michelle always connected with people and was ever quick to smile and laugh. Annette described how Michelle frequently talked about her love for her students and her school. Annette also expressed how Michelle was wired to be a mother and was a gifted singer and musician.

Annette saw Michelle as a precious servant of God. Her eulogy concluded with a verse that reflects Michelle wonderfully: "And let the peace of Christ rule in your hearts, to which indeed you were called in one body. And be thankful" (Col. 3:15).

Then I stood to speak. An inner boldness came over me that was beyond my own capacity. I began by letting everyone know that Michelle had asked me to deliver the eulogy. I told them how she instructed me to do two things: (1) say good things about her and (2) share the gospel. This was an easy commission to carry out.

I then let the people in on a secret. Michelle often told me that she didn't think she was making much difference in people's lives. She couldn't have been more wrong. I often told her that she might not realize her impact until she got to heaven.

When I was preparing the eulogy, I asked myself, "What does Scripture say when referring to the kind of impact Christians are to make?" I chose to focus on Matthew 5:14-16: "You are the light of the world. A city set on a hill cannot be hidden. Nor do people light a lamp and put it under a basket, but on a stand, and it gives light to all in the house. In the same way, let your light shine before others, so that they may see your good works and give glory to your Father who is in heaven" Christians are to be light to a dark world so that our actions bring glory to God.

Michelle's influence came in four categories. The first was her impact as a teacher. It wasn't by accident. The soccer star of a few decades ago, Pelé, had it right when he said, "Success is no accident. It is hard work, perseverance, learning, studying, sacrifice and most of all, love of what you are doing or learning to do."[17] Over the years, she followed this advice and spent countless hours perfecting her craft.

For instance, she went above and beyond the call of duty by earning two master's degrees, spending her summers preparing for the coming year, and always making it a point to pray daily for her students. What was done in secret would now be publicly recognized. I was in awe as I read the Facebook posts that came from students and parents regarding the impact Michelle had made. Below are a few of those statements.[18]

Student #1

More than anything, you showed us how to love. You demonstrated this when you showed us pictures of your daughter Faith each week. It was clear that you put all your heart and soul not only into your lesson plans, but into our projects. You taught us

---

17 Quoted in https://www.brainyquote.com/quotes/keywords/hard_work.html.
18 Some of the statements have been edited.

that we should work our hardest and put our passion into these things. You encouraged us to pursue happiness.

Thank you for supporting me when I moved on to college and was far away from home. Thank you for checking in on me from time to time and encouraging me in all my work. Thank you for giving me resources when I had to take a Spanish placement test and had learned so many new things since my last day of Spanish. Thank you for being so kind and so compassionate to me and to every one of your students. Thank you, Señora Orr, for being the person that you were.

Student #2

As a student you have no clue how close you can get to a teacher. That teacher can not only be your teacher, but a leader, a friend and someone you can count on. I was given the sad news that my Spanish teacher from high school at CSA has passed away. She always could make me smile. During my senior year, I was her student teacher as well as her student. It allowed me to understand her so much better. When I left high school, and moved on to college the bond between us started becoming stronger. She always loved her students. During my Spanish years, she always loved making *tu mama* jokes, letting my crazy Spanish class give her a hard time. My Spanish group wrote our first book and put together a crazy movie and we always had big events planned and they always seemed to wow the community. Most importantly, we have many memories that none of us will ever forget. Myself and a few others, during graduation weekend were reflecting back on so many memories that we all shared with her. I am sure going to miss her and seeing her as I walk into the doors of CSA.

.

Student #3

I love this woman more that words can explain. She was such an amazing person and always went out of her way to help others including myself. Even when I wasn't in her class anymore she always greeted me with a smile and would say *Hola Yami* or *Hola mija.* Words cannot explain how much it hurts she was not only my facilitator, but she was a part of my family at CSA.

Parent #1

I have a 17-year-old daughter who rarely sheds a tear or at least no one knows when she does. Today, her tears fell freely at the loss of a beautiful teacher and mentor. Michelle Orr was that and much more. Our hearts are broken for Tim Orr and Faith. Thank you, Michelle. It's a treasure in today's world to find a teacher who prays for your child and fights for their best interest.

Church Member

Second, Michelle was also a great church member. She was known for her love for God, her love for prayer, and her love for worship. What many did not know until this day was from where this love came.

Her commitment to God's kingdom and His church shined brightly the entire time I knew her. As a matter of fact, this is one of the things that first endeared her to me. Before we were married, I had already committed to serve as a pastor. My own pastor, Randy Ballard, gave me some great advice when I began looking for a wife. Knowing my vocational goals, he recommended that I look for someone who would complement me in ministry. Michelle was the perfect person.

She followed me to East Chicago to plant a church and then to Bloomfield to pastor another church. These were difficult places to serve, but my wife worked alongside me joyfully and faithfully. I watched her serve as a mother figure for years to kids in East Chicago who had no mom in their life.

I explained that day that her love for God and her love for children didn't just suddenly emerge when she was an adult. Rather, it stemmed from an experience when she was just 5 years old—when she was in that Sunday school class. Even at her young age, the music impacted her deeply, and the lyrics stayed with her long after.

A Great Mother

Third, Michelle was a great mother. For years she had wanted a biological child but couldn't. But in 2009, she got the opportunity to be a mother when we adopted Faith. It was an answer to a prayer of many years for this privilege. Michelle took full advantage of this opportunity.

A Great Wife

Fourth, I finished by telling what kind of wife Michelle was. Many people commented over the years how she talked about her love for Faith and me. And she showed it in multiple ways over the years. Her prayers, support, and encouragement were a source of strength for our family. When she died, I began to realize how often I had turned to her when things were difficult. Now, with her no longer there, I said that my focus would be even more centered on God, who is the ultimate source of my strength.

After the service, I ventured outside to speak with those who attended. This was quite a job, given all the people who had come to pay their respects. I saw their love for Michelle as they shook hands, hugged me, or just delivered a kind word about how much they appreciated her. Friends, church family, neighbors, students, and staff came together that day to show their appreciation.

While Michelle never understood the impact she had made, I saw and felt that impact as I greeted every person who came that day. In a sense, they were jointly confirming what had already been confirmed in heaven when Michelle was whisked into eternity: "Well done, good and faithful servant!"

Why Did Michelle Die?

When Michelle passed away, given her age and her sudden death, an autopsy was done. I wondered if there was something the doctors could have done to prevent her death. Several weeks passed until I received the results. I discovered that the cause of death was heart failure, not cancer. The coroner told me that he didn't find anything else abnormal.

What was I to make of her death? I have no conclusive evidence to back up the claim that I am about to make, but I believe Michelle did in fact have cancer and that God had healed it. I know of no other reason why the earlier tests showed what they did, when only weeks later there was virtually no trace of disease.

Whatever the case, Michelle was given a few more months on earth to enjoy before she received her eternal reward. This time gave her and Faith the opportunity to enjoy the Disney trip, which Michelle always wanted to share with Faith. Because God loved Michelle so much, He blessed her with this precious memory.

What's more, through the cancer scare, I was emotionally prepared for her passing. The many "what if" talks we had helped me plan what I should do if she didn't make it. Even in the mist of devastating circumstances, God was extending His grace.

Nine

I Needed Help

After Michelle's funeral, Faith, Mike, and I drove home from Michigan to prepare for Michelle's memorial that would take place a little over a week later. It was late when we finally arrived, and Faith was more than ready for bed. I carried in the suitcase and Faith walked beside me as we went to the front door. The last time I had darkened the door was a few days earlier, when I had received the phone call that Michelle had passed away.

When I escorted Faith to her room to kiss her goodnight, she asked me the same painful question she would ask repeatedly over the coming months: "When is Mommy coming home?" I just told her softly that Mommy was in heaven and wasn't coming home then kissed her on the cheek as she got into bed. It was late, so she didn't respond with a follow-up question.

The next few months were rough for Faith. She didn't cry much but she clearly was sad. Faith and her mom had been very close. Their bond strengthened as they spent many, many hours doing things like homework, playing, and reading books. Suddenly, all that was no more.

I alone was not enough to give Faith what she needed. She needed others to sew into her life. So Faith's family, school, church, and caregivers all stepped in to help provide what she needed.

Faith's Family

The Bible speaks a lot about family. The family was the first institution God constructed. After Adam was created, God said Adam needed a helpmate, so he created Eve. The two of them came together and became one flesh (i.e. married) and out of that union came children. Together they became a family. The family, in turn, becomes the building block of society as several families come together to form a larger community.

Families are our primary source of security, stability, identity, and instruction. They are to be places where each person receives complete acceptance and love. The first institution that should rally around someone facing difficulty is that person's family. In the situation that Faith was experiencing, aunts, uncles, grandmas, and grandpas played a pivotal role.

As her father, I am to train, equip, and instruct Faith. According to Proverbs, I am to "[t]rain up a child in the way he should go; even when he is old he will not depart from it" (Prov. 26:4). My responsibility is also to ensure Faith is taken care of properly, getting the love and care she needs.

Therefore, I provided Faith with opportunities to build relationships with family. She needs grandparents and aunts and uncles in her life, from both sets of families. Most importantly, I am committed to maintaining relationships with Michelle's family so Faith can continue to benefit from having them in her life. She needs to know Michelle's extended family well. This involves getting together for Christmas and spending part of her summer vacation with them. I love it when I hear Faith talk about the fun times she has with them. These relationships give her the love and support she needs.

There is one relationship that is vital for Faith above the others, and that is her relationship with her Aunt Roberta. She is the closest to a mother figure Faith has that is a blood relative. Right now, if something happens to me, Roberta gets custody. Therefore, building this bond is important. In the future, if I remarry, I hope that my wife assumes that role over time. Until then, Roberta serves that role.

Church Family

One of the best things a church can do through times like this is offer pastoral care. The church is to be led by shepherds who know, feed, lead, and protect the sheep. Done properly, pastoral care is a natural outcome of building strong leaders who shepherd the flock of God. I was so grateful to Terrace Lake Church, which is our home church in Columbus, exemplified this type of leadership.

Many of the ladies of the church cared for Faith, surrounded by other children, in their homes. Faith got to swim, ride bikes, and play in parks. My daughter also got to cuddle and read, play dress up, eat meals, and smother others with hugs. They gave her the physical touch and positive words she needed! Faith also opened up and told these ladies how much she missed her mommy. They in turn listened and offered their support.

My friend Adrienne will never forget a conversation she had after picking Faith up from one of her teacher's homes. Adrienne's mother was visiting from Ohio and her daughter, Tess, was in the car with them. After her mother greeted Faith, Faith asked who she was, as they had never met before. Adrienne's mother said to Faith, "I'm her mom," pointing to Adrienne. This prompted Faith to point to everyone in the car, making all the connections, such as daughter, mom, and grandma. Faith really got a kick out of it. She has a tremendous sense of humor.

This cheerful exchange was followed by a somber moment. Faith told Adrienne's mother that her own mom had died. She responded by giving Faith some needed encouragement—and the exchange turned out to be reciprocal. Not only did this family minister to Faith, but Faith ministered to them.

The church also gave Faith some books that help children deal with death, such as *Tess's Tree* and *Tear Soup*. The children's ministry kept in contact with Faith's school, giving updates and coordinating some of her needs with Sydell, Faith's principal.

All involved had a detailed plan to ensure her needs were met. Hannah, the physical therapist who works with Faith at her school, also served as the special needs coordinator at the church. Faith didn't require many special services, but these helpers employed certain techniques to communicate with Faith about what she was supposed to do.

Transitioning from the K-1 class to the 2-4 class, my daughter did quite well. A third person was placed in the room to help and encourage Faith as needed. Since Hannah already worked with Faith at school, Terrace Lake used the school's behavioral plan so that the lessons she was learning could be reinforced at church.

After Michelle passed away, we received meals every day for the first two months. This was in addition to the daily dinners that were delivered to our home during all the time Michelle was sick and believed to have had cancer.

With all this generosity from my church family, I think I ate better than I ever had in my life. It was not uncommon to have a lot of leftovers. After a week or two, I wised up and began to freeze some of the meals, turning two months' worth of meals into three.

Often the family bringing the meal would stay and talk for a while. I needed to hear the genuine love and concern these friends had for Faith and me. Sometimes being reminded that what you are feeling is normal is what I needed to make it through the day. Faith also was blessed by these visits.

The church also organized a work day for us. When we were married, Michelle would sometimes ask me to fix things around the house. I usually told her I would get to it but often never did. I seem to have a special gift for procrastination in this area. A week before the men from the church came over, Billy, the pastor's brother, dropped by to see what needed repairing. He was amazing. I think he needed two sheets of paper to write everything down. The bathtub needed to be caulked, the fence repaired, the shed painted and organized, the gate repaired, and the landscaping tackled.

One of the things Faith liked most was going to the park with her mom. So the church honored this memory by setting up a nice playground in our backyard.

Terrace Lake has many engineers as members, and one of them, Eric, helped lead the project. Engineers tend to think mathematically and methodologically, a fact that was evident in front of my home that day. I live in a cul-de-sac, which has a large area to park cars. When I walked outside to visit with the people working, I saw three or four rows of cars parked outside my door. They were all perfectly organized, each car exactly two feet from the vehicle beside it. When I pointed it out to a few guys, they laughed along with me. The precise arrangement wasn't planned. It just came naturally, I guess.

Taylorsville Elementary School

Taylorsville Elementary School, under the leadership of Principal Sydell Gant, also played an important role in Faith's life after her mom died. But the school's impact on Faith was nothing new. During the fall of 2014, Faith entered the school as a kindergartener, a level she went through twice. Given Faith's age and disability, I was concerned about her riding the bus. I called Mrs. Gant, who invited me to stop by the school and talk. This was the first time we had met. She addressed my worries, and I was confident that she really cared about the students.

That sense of care became even more evident. Dropping Faith off the first few days, I noticed that the person greeting everyone at the door knew Faith by name. A day or two later, I talked briefly with the same lady. She shared with me the few interactions she had already had with Faith. This woman knew Faith personally and was familiar with her needs.

The next day, as I was walking Faith to the gym to drop her off, the custodian walked by and called Faith by name. He commented how he enjoyed interacting with her. The same was true with both the office and support staff. Within the first week, several staff members not only knew who Faith was, but seemed to care about her and her success as a student.

These brief examples illustrate a well-developed learning community. It was clear to me that the other students were receiving the same care and concern. Each staff member was playing an integral part in meeting student needs, establishing relational connections, and educating the child with the goal of fostering his or her success.

This connection was extra important after Michelle passed away. So many of the staff had already built a relationship with Faith and possessed a genuine love for her. For example, Mrs. Kessler asked how old Faith was going to be on her birthday. When Faith responded, "I am not having a birthday because my mommy's not here," her teacher told that her mother loved her and was proud of her. A big grin from Faith followed.

This kind and thoughtful response reflected the school's plan to nurture Faith. I received the following note from Mrs. Gant:

As a school community, Taylorsville, the school with Heart, is committed to honoring Michelle's legacy by supporting Faith in her education. Faith's growth was the source of Michelle's pride in her daughter, and we are privileged to carry forward Faith's academic, social, and emotional progress. The bond between mother and daughter can never be replaced, and through the grieving process, Faith has reflected qualities of her mother—her strength, her determination, her persistence. When the emotions would come, we could wrap our arms around this sweet child, standing in for Michelle, as only a mother can do, consoling and loving a child in need. We cannot understand the why behind this path for Faith. Instead, we trust the plan laid out before them [MICHELLE AND FAITH?], allowing ourselves to be used in supporting them along this journey.

Given the amount of time children spend under their care, schools have an opportunity to make a great impact. What a joy it was for me to know that Faith was receiving the love and support she needed at school to get through this tough time in her life.

Help at Home

Finally, I want to mention the key role played by Faith's caregivers, through a tremendous organization called Help at Home. A lady named Jerri Ann, the daughter of one of Michelle's former school colleagues, ensures that Faith's needs are met. The great thing is that both Jerri Ann and her mother knew and loved Faith even before we chose this agency.

Every day, Faith and her mom spent two to three hours doing homework, reading, and playing. Without Help at Home there, doing so much of what Michelle used to do, Faith would have felt a much deeper void.

Conclusion

These are the members of my supporting cast, all of whom play an important role in Faith's development. The quote popularized years ago that says, "It takes a village to raise a child," is true. By myself, I simply could not give my daughter all that she needed. Thank God that her family, school, church, and caregivers all have stepped in to help Faith along life's journey.

Ten

The last time Faith saw her mom was the day Michelle died—Faith was sitting in her lap, trying to wake her up. During the following months, Faith often asked me why her mother didn't wake up. Replaying what happened to me over and over, my daughter wanted answers. Every time I had to field the question, it was hard to shield my anguish. I just hugged her and reminded her that her mom was in heaven and one day they would see each other again.

Why Return to Disney

I reflected deeply on how to help Faith overcome this memory. I didn't want this to be how she remembered her mom. I wanted her to think of all the fun they had together. The longer I pondered what to do, the more my choice became obvious. Faith and I would return to Disney World.

The last time we were there we enjoyed a week of celebration. Michelle had no cancer! We thought we were going to be together for years and years to come. We all had a blast. It was an experience we will never forget.

Last time, Michelle and our friend Zoe planned the trip. This time it was just Zoe. I am not a detail person at all, so I asked her to plan the trip for me. I told her a few things I wanted, and she did the rest.

To prepare Faith, she and I looked at the pictures of our prior trip. We mentally walked through being at the Magic Kingdom, Epcot Center, and Animal Kingdom. I reminded her of the Dumbo ride, the place where we drank the many flavors of soft drinks, and all the beautiful animals we saw. Every time we discussed it, Faith's face lit up.

The weeks flew by until there were just mere days before we would head south for our Disney experience. Faith and I were so excited. I knew the significance that this trip might have in her life.

More Bad News

On the Friday before the Monday Faith and I were to leave for our trip, my mother was at work when her boss told her that someone was in the breakroom who wanted to speak with her. She was given no more details. When she entered the room, a detective told her he had some difficult news. She braced herself, thinking that perhaps her 94-year-old mother had died. Instead, he told her that my brother, Shannon, two years my junior, had just been killed by a drunken driver.

The truck had hit Shannon's vehicle broadside, dragging it several feet and pinning it against a building. The other driver fled the scene. Shannon's neck was broken. He died instantly. The news devastated my mother. She and Shannon had remained very close over the years. Now he was gone.

My mom called my brother, Josh, and his wife, Stacey, who came to her workplace. They hugged and cried together. Then they all went to my grandmother's house to tell her about a loss that no one thought possible. Her grandson was dead.

That day, I was to meet Mike and Jody as well as Pastor Danny at the country club for lunch, followed by a round of golf. I arrived early, sipping a Diet Coke. My phone rang, and it was Josh. I sensed a trembling in his voice. Then he uttered the same words that my mother-in-law had said when she informed me about Michelle: "I don't know how to tell you this." I closed my eyes and braced myself for whatever it was. Mike and Jody arrived just as I got the news. "Oh my God, oh my God," was how I responded.

When I hung up the phone, Jody gently recommended that I text my friend Sydell, the principal at Faith's school, to let her know what had happened. Jody would pick Faith up and let her stay all night with her family as I made the two-hour trip to be with the rest of the family. I pulled out of the country club in stunned disbelief. I couldn't even pray.

Shannon and I grew up together. We were only two years apart chronologically but were worlds apart in our personalities. Nonetheless, we spent a lot of time together until I entered the teenage years and found friends my age.

As I drove, I recalled an instance when I was about 10, and each of us had a pony horse. The horses were also great for pretend play. Often, we dressed up in our cowboy suits, complete with other attire, such as cap guns and boots. We imagined we were the Lone Ranger and Tonto. The Lone Ranger was always my choice.

We also played a lot in the holler. For those who didn't grow up in Indiana, a holler is a valley with a creek at the bottom. We played there for hours on end. We were typical boys who just loved to play outside. (Video games had yet to come on the scene.)

Even though we had grown far apart through the decades, the emotional bond built while we were kids was still there. Now Shannon was gone. There was no chance to say goodbye. No more chances to rekindle our friendship. I would never see him again.

When I arrived at my younger brother Joshua's house, the rest of my immediate family was already there. We were beside ourselves, huddled together at the kitchen table. Just four months earlier we had lost Michelle. Now Shannon.

When my mom walked into the room, she immediately came over to hug me, and we both broke down. Then she asked me why Michelle and

Shannon had to die so close together. I had no answers. I wasn't trained for those kinds of questions.

Shannon's Funeral

The following day my mom, Josh, Stacey, and a few other family members went to the funeral home. This was the last time the family would be able to see Shannon, given that his wish was to be cremated. Because of the severity of his injuries, the funeral home had wrapped him in a blanket from the neck down.

The family decided to have his memorial service that Monday, the same day Faith and I were scheduled to travel to Disney. The funeral would be earlier than our departure time, so I could preach the funeral and keep my promise to my daughter.

At the service, many people came to pay Shannon, who had been very well-liked, the respect he deserved. It was standing room only. Some mourners had to be turned away because the building couldn't hold them.

I preached my best under the circumstances, honoring my brother's memory and sharing the gospel. When the service ended, Faith and I got in a car and began the long drive to Florida. I would rather have waited, but we really couldn't, given the circumstances.

Off to Disney

Starting the car, I saw Faith's smiling face in the rearview mirror. She said, "I am ready to go to Disney, Daddy!" It reminded me that the reason for this trip was to keep the smile on her face. I had feared that Faith would become bitter because of what had happened. I certainly had because of the tragedies I endured as a child. At the time, I hated my life, hated myself, and hated God. My situation wasn't fair, and I became very bitter. I didn't want that to happen to Faith. I was willing to do anything to prevent this.

It took two full days to get to Disney. We weren't in a hurry. During the drive, I hid my grief for Faith's sake. This was to be a fun experience to help remind my daughter of the good times she had enjoyed with Michelle. I didn't want my grief to spoil what was planned.

While driving, I did a lot of praying, but I felt as if I was going through the motions. The first night at our hotel, Faith and I ordered pizza and ate while watching a television show. An hour later, Faith was in bed for the night, which gave me a lot of time to think.

To sort through the pain, I grabbed a pen and paper. Journaling helps me to process things I would rather suppress. It serves the same purpose as cleaning up my office. It is difficult for me to get any work done if my work space is cluttered. However, if I have it cleaned up and organized, I can complete my work.

That night I needed to de-clutter my mind. I was hurting. I needed to begin the long process of healing by unpacking my pain onto the sheet of paper and pouring my heart out to God. This is never easy for me. My natural tendency is to intellectualize. Journaling helps me to access my thoughts, then process them. Transferring my thoughts from my mind to the paper, I avoid suppressing my feelings.

But I needed more than this. I needed God's strength. The Psalmists poured their hearts out to God and found refuge in Him. For example, Psalm 62:8 encourages believers to do just that: "Trust in him at all times, … pour out your heart before him; God is a refuge for us." My journaling helped me transfer my thoughts from my mind, to the paper, and finally to God. This is how I could be strong for Faith. God had to be my refuge in my time of pain.

Certainly, everything wasn't wonderful after I had finished that night. I was still hurting. But I did receive what I needed at that moment. Surviving difficult times required me to approach God as my refuge daily, if not hourly, even minute by minute. My ultimate solace is found in my relationship with God. Journaling helps me make this a reality.

Disney Again!

The next day we made it to Disney. To build Faith's anticipation, I shared memories of our experience from six months earlier—where we ate, where we stayed, and what rides we enjoyed in the park. The memories resonated with Faith, who shared some details she remembered.

Despite all this, my mood was downcast, until we drove up to the entrance. The familiar sign that hovers over the road said, "Walt Disney World, where dreams come true." Mickey Mouse is featured on one side of the road while Minnie Mouse is featured on the other. The sign triggered my thoughts of prior trips. One of my fondest memories of Disney occurred when I was a little boy overtaken with enchantment when I first walked into the park. Everywhere I looked, I saw smiles. They set the tone for the entire day.

We immediately walked past the shops and into the park where the rides were located. As our excitement percolated to a fever pitch, I was trying to recreate the enchantment that Faith had enjoyed when she went to Disney with her mom and relive, to some degree, the many precious moments that those two had experienced. I wanted Faith to see some of the same shows, ride the same rides, and eat at the same restaurants.

We began our four-day vacation by going to Hollywood Studios. The first character we saw was Doc McStuffins, about whom Michelle and Faith used to talk a lot. This provided me with the opportunity to help Faith reminisce about the times she and her mom watched the show together. After visiting another favorite of Michelle and Faith, *Disney Junior – Live on Stage*, we capped the day off with a dinner at *50's Prime Time Cafe Dinner*.

The next day was Thanksgiving, my favorite holiday of the year. Michelle had always taken the opportunity to show off her culinary skills by cooking my favorite food. I was guaranteed to have baked beans, sweet potatoes, deviled eggs, and meat loaf (as I was not a fan of turkey). This time, however, our food choice was different.

Faith and I didn't go to the restaurant where we had our reservation. Instead, we opted for the *Tusker House*. The main draw for me was the character dining. Faith got her picture with Mickey Mouse, Goofy, and Daffy Duck. Faith really enjoyed herself. She is a natural in front of the camera, so the Disney characters' willingness to take pictures with her made her day.

On Friday we went to Disney World so that Faith could enjoy many of the same rides she had experienced with her mother the last time. My highlight on Friday was getting together with my cousin Jeff. He and his family happened to be visiting Disney at the same time. On Friday night he came over for a visit after his kids went to bed. Growing up, I usually spent Thanksgiving with his family every year. I would go to their house sometime in the early afternoon, would eat supper with them, then play several hands of Euchar, with some football in between. These were fond memories.

So it was a treat to reminisce with Jeff about old times. Having just lost Michelle and Shannon, I needed to regain some sense of family. This experience filled my emotional tank. God knew what I needed.

The next day was our last at Disney. We spent the morning at Epcot Center and went to a few shows, but Faith had reached her limit. It was a fun trip, but it was time to go.

Conclusion

On the two-day return trip, we had many hours to talk, and it was clear that Faith had enjoyed a great time—my prayers had been answered. My goal during the trip was to cement the great memories Faith had with my wife while at Disney the last time. When Faith shared the highlights of this trip with me, she pointed out the similar experiences she and her mom had enjoyed last time. Our trip to the Magic Kingdom had been a success. I was grateful.

Eleven

Michelle's death took everyone by surprise, including me. But some things had been set in motion long ago that provided what Faith needed in Michelle's absence. My new situation was overwhelming at first, but the more I thought about it, the more I realized that prior life experiences had prepared me for it.

Growing up with deformities caused me an almost unbearable sense of shame, which God replaced with His love and honor. The tyranny of rejection forced me to go deeper in my understanding of the gospel, causing me to root my security in my relationship with Christ instead of other things. I am a much better father today than I would have been without this training ground of affliction. Three things stand out in my mind because of that training.

The Power of Connection

Nothing could bring me greater joy than to know that I am bringing God's grace and love to Faith. Since Faith no longer had a mother, she needed a deep connection with her father. Fortunately, provisions for that connection had already been made. Often when the mother dies while the child is young, the father must begin to learn to connect with his daughter on the deep level she needs.

My preparation for this connection began the day Faith was born. Our financial obligations played a part in this. Because Michelle made more money than I did, we decided that I should stay home with Faith the first few years while Michelle went to work. This allowed me to establish a father and daughter bond that proved to be pivotal later.

The bond began to form almost immediately after we brought her home. One night, as I was feeding her in our living room, long after Michelle had gone to bed, I looked in Faith's eyes, and it was if she was saying, "This is my daddy." I had the chance to offer this little girl in my arms something I never could get from my earthly father. The bond we built from the beginning was special, and being home with Faith for those first three years helped ensure that it would be strong for years to come.

The Power of Gratitude

There is something about the power of gratitude. It is one of the keys to successful parenting. A parent who is happy, healthy, optimistic, and less stressed when life's challenges come about will do a better job raising emotionally healthy kids. Given the difficult circumstances Faith and I found ourselves in, living out this principle was foundational.

The foundation of my gratitude begins with my salvation. At the risk of sounding churchy, Jesus died for my sins and rose from the dead so I could be made right before God. Since my salvation is a gift from God that I couldn't earn, only accepted by faith alone, gratitude was my only rational response.

In an article titled "Freshly Fueled Grace," Scotty Smith records a prayer of gratitude that captures this spirit.

As my Savior and Redeemer, Jesus, I adore you for living in my place and dying in my place; for sins forgiven and righteousness given; for victory over death and grace for life; for your steadfast love and daily mercies; for citizenship in heaven and a place in your kingdom; for the hope of glory and the glory of the gospel... just to name a few![19]

Over time, these truths became real to me as I meditated on them and asked God to illuminate them to me by His Holy Spirit. This meant treasuring every day what Christ has done on the cross and in the resurrection. I found that this kind of mindfulness about all I had in Christ led me to walk in the joy and victory that flow from my salvation. I saw the power of sin broken in my life, felt an increased sense of the joy of the Lord, and understood through personal experience that Christ had forgiven and justified me. This is the basis for my gratitude.

However, the same God who bestowed salvation upon His children is the same God who bestows other gifts. After my conversion, I began to read the Bible and discover what it says about the family. This fostered a desire for a wife and kids. During the chapel service in 1991, I believed that God had promised me this would happen. Two years later, I was married. God had kept the first part of His promise.

However, it took 16 more years for us to have a daughter. By that time, Michelle and I had given up this dream. Yet God brought Faith into our lives as a gift to raise. We were determined to train her to be a young woman who would one day make an impact.

I still keep this motivation in mind. Every day I wake up grateful for the opportunity to raise this young lady. Despite her special needs, she is not a burden. I consider it an honor and privilege to be her daddy.

The Power of a Heart Devoted to God

Faith needed a dad with a heart for God. But what does having a heart for God look like? The Psalmist captures it quite well when he says,

---

19 Scotty Smith, "Freshly Fueled Gratitude," April 22, 2016, The Gospel Coalition, https://blogs.thegospelcoalition.org/scottysmith/2016/04/22/freshly-fueled-gratitude/, accessed November 4, 2017.

For God alone, O my soul, wait in silence, for my hope is from him. He only is my rock and my salvation, my fortress; I shall not be shaken. On God rests my salvation and my glory; my mighty rock, my refuge is God (Psalm 62:5-8).

To have a heart for God means having a single-minded devotion to God.

Years ago, I discovered that the more I drew closer to God, the more he transformed my life. Nothing too terribly profound. However, the more I was transformed into Christ's image, the greater impact I made in the lives of others, which meant the more I could later nurture the spiritual life of my daughter.

I have faced significant obstacles in reaching that goal. Before God sent us Faith, I needed Him to do a work in my heart. Given the broken relationship I had with my earthly father, I had a distorted understanding of my heavenly Father. Though my creedal understanding of God was thoroughly orthodox, I still saw Him as somewhat of a tyrant whom I could never please. Consequently, God took me through a process that allowed me a firm grasp of His love for me. Without God moving in my life as He did and helping me to understand His love for me, it would have been difficult for me to have a father's heart for Faith.

God had graciously developed in me a strong relationship with Himself, enabling me to survive the experience of losing my wife and then my brother in quick succession. The resources that I drew upon daily to keep my schedule and still have time to be a single dad take daily deposits of God's grace. Past hardship paved the way for me to be transformed into the father Faith needs. There is something about going through difficult times that produces transformation.

Conclusion

My past prepared me to be the father that Faith needs. In the next three chapters, I write a series of letters from a father offering advice to a young daughter who has just lost her mother.

The letters are divided into three categories. The first series of letters focus on her mom. My purpose is to share tidbits about her mother that will help keep her memory alive. I don't want Faith to ever forget the blessing that her mom was in her life.

The second series of letters focuses on encouraging Faith. She will need much encouragement through the years as she lives without her mom. My goal in these letters is to help keep her smiling.

The third and last series of letters focuses on fatherly advice. Many things will come her way for which she will need the wisdom of her father.

Twelve

Letters About Her Mom

I Couldn't Wake Mommy Up

Here is the letter I gave to Faith shortly before our second trip to Disney World:

Dear Faith,

Ever since your mom's untimely death, you occasionally refer to what happened the day you mom passed away. You and your mom were so close, and I hate that your earthly relationship had to end the way it did.

I have been thinking a lot about what to do. I don't want the memory of her death to be cemented in your mind. It is not how I want you to remember your mom. When you think of her, I want you to think about all the good times you had and how much she loved you. There were so many good memories that you can reflect on that will tell a more accurate story of her and the relationship you two shared.

Despite her untimely death, never forget that God placed her in your life for a certain period of time for a reason. He knew beforehand you two would only be together for six years. It didn't take Him by surprise. During that short period of time, He wanted her to contribute to your life that will pay dividends the rest of your life.

Because we all live in a fallen world, there is one thing you can be assured. There are many pleasant as well as painful experiences that lay ahead. When the painful or difficult times come, and they will, remember not to forget the good memories. They will carry you through many troubled waters.

Your mom used to take a lot of pictures of you, and I mean lots. She wanted to cherish every moment she had with you, and have a snapshot of all those good times. These memories are like pictures the stay in your mind for you to view. You can replay them anytime you want.

By continuing to reflect on the good times, it will help to cushion your loss. Fortunately, your mom is not gone forever. You will see her one day, again, when you get to heaven. Until then, keep those memories close to your heart. There will be times in your life where these memories serve as a lifeboat during troubled times. They will be an anchor during a storm.

Too often, our minds become fixated on what is wrong. Keeping these memories alive helps you to reflect on what is right about the world. To help with this, I have arranged another trip to Disney World. This was the last major fun trip you and your mom did together.

We leave for the trip next week. My plan is to revisit every fun ride, event, or show that you and your mom did together just a few months ago. My prayer is that those will be cemented in your mind the rest of your life.

It will be Thanksgiving weekend, so it might be a little busy toward the latter part of the week.

You are probably wondering how we are going to get there. Don't worry. I plan to drive down, because I know how much you hate flying.

I should also add that there is one more reason for taking this trip. It is important that we continue to make memories together. One of the fondest memories [I had] was when I went to Disney World as a kid. Occasionally, I pull out the pictures of my cousin Jeff and me, sporting our sunglasses and cool pose, strutting our stuff before the camera. I still remember riding Space Mountain eight times in a row. The first time was scary, but the last seven times were a blast.

In the coming years, there will be plenty of daddy/daughter times, I am sure. Disney will be our vacation spot for years to come I am sure. I want us to continue to nurture the bond we have together.

Remember to reflect on the good times you had with your mom. Try to remember what it was like when mommy was sitting next to you while you were on one of the rides. Remember the smile on her face. The smile represents her love for you. These are the kinds of things I want you to remember when you think of mommy.

Hugs and kisses,

Daddy

• • •

Mommy's First Anniversary

Dear Faith,

I woke up this morning and began my normal routines. I begin by looking at my phone so I can access the apt that contains my daily calendar. When I did, I noticed the date at the top. It read

June 27, 2017, which meant one year ago to the day your mommy passed away. I wasn't ready for it. I realized afresh how much I truly missed her and I know you do too.

Now, every year on this day we will be reminded that your mommy is no longer with us. Her memory will probably fade somewhat, but her impact on your life won't. I plan to rekindle those memories every year with thoughts of her impact on your life and where she is spending eternity. She is with Jesus and one day we will spend eternity with her.

I thought about how we should remember your mommy each year now. I decided we would celebrate it. For eternity, your mom is in heaven. Heaven is a real place where God dwells. It is a place where the toils and trials that we experience on earth will be no more. It is a place where God "will wipe away every tear from [our] eyes, and death shall be no more, neither shall there be mourning, nor crying, nor pain anymore, for the former things have passed away" (Rev. 21:3-4). You will never again feel the pain of losing a loved one. There will be no more hurt and no more pain.

The world there is truly spectacular. It is a place that is filled with the "glory of God, its radiance like a most rare jewel, like a jasper, clear as crystal" (Rev. 21:11b). Christians will dwell there together in perfect unity. There will also be angels performing their duties to bring continual glory to God.

The walls of the city are "built with jasper ... while the city [is] pure gold, like clear glass. The foundations of the wall of the city [are] adorned with every kind of jewel. The first [is] jasper, the second sapphire, the third agate, the fourth emerald, [20] the fifth onyx, the sixth carnelian, the seventh chrysolite, the eighth beryl, the ninth topaz, the tenth chrysoprase, the eleventh jacinth, the twelfth amethyst" (Rev. 21:19-20). I am not even sure what some of the jewels really look like, but I know it is wonderful.

The city gates are made of pearls, while the streets are made of "pure gold, like transparent glass" (Rev. 21:21b).

However, the most important part of heaven is that it is the dwelling place of God. There is "no temple in the city, for its temple is the Lord God the Almighty and the Lamb. [23] And the city has no need of sun or moon to shine on it, for the glory of God gives it light, and its lamp is the Lamb. [24] By its light will the nations walk, and the kings of the earth will bring their glory into it, [25] and its gates will never be shut by day—and there will be no night there. [26] They will bring into it the glory and the honor of the nations. [27] But nothing unclean will ever enter it, nor anyone who does what is detestable or false ..." (Rev. 21:22-27b).

The most important takeaway about heaven you need to remember is who is allowed to enter. Not everyone goes to heaven. As a matter of fact, most people, by their own choice motivated by rebellious hearts, do not spend eternity in heaven. They refuse to see their need for a savior. Instead, heaven is a place where only those who enter are "those [whose names are] written in the Lamb's book of life" (Rev. 21:27:c).

Your mommy's name was put into this book the day she trusted Christ at the age of 7. She went to children's church just like you. One day when she heard the message of the gospel she repented and trusted Christ for her salvation. I am praying the same for you.

This is why we went out for dinner tonight to celebrate mommy's first anniversary in heaven. Oftentimes the anniversary of a person's death is something sad because you relive the loss. There is a loss on our end. Please don't ever try to drown out those feelings when you think about your mom. But allow me to recommend that you also ponder the reality of where she is now. She is in a place where there is no pain, no sickness, and no heartache. She is experiencing joyous contentment because she is in the presence of God for eternity.

The best part of all of this, is that one day she will be with her forever, never to be separated again. I have asked you what you thought mommy is doing right now in heaven. You told me that she is worshipping, singing and dancing. One day you will be worshipping, singing, and dancing right beside her. You too will be face to face with Jesus enjoying God's presence because of what Christ has done. Therefore, we will celebrate mommy's anniversary in heaven every year on this day.

Hugs and kisses,

Daddy

• • •

Mommy's Devotional Life

Dear Faith,

If there is one takeaway from your mommy's life that you should try to emulate, it is her devotion to Jesus. The entire time I was married to her, I saw her devotion firsthand. It wasn't a religious performance she was putting on in public, then became another person in private. Your mommy was the real deal.

What nurtured her ongoing devotion to Jesus was her time she spent with Him every day, reading and studying the Bible and praying. She considered the Bible her daily bread and looked to Job 23:12 for inspiration. It says, "I have not departed from the commandment of his lips; I have treasured the words of his mouth more than my portion of food." She usually read her Bible in the evening or nighttime.

Because she saw God's Word as her daily bread, she knew she needed to read it every day. Like King David in the Old Testament, she saw it as God's wisdom that guided her thoughts and decisions, making it a "lamp to [her] feet and a light to [her] path" (Psalm 119:105). She knew that when God's wisdom was applied, she would be changed by it. Consequently, she wanted to apply God's truth so she would be salt and light in the lives of others.

She also saw God's Word as the source that nourished her soul. (Deuteronomy 8:3, Matthew 4:4). While physical food like mashed potatoes, your favorite food, nourishes the physical body, God's Word nourishes the soul. Your mom understood that when she read and studied God's Word, it was "living and active, sharper than any two-edged sword, piercing to the division of soul and of spirit, of joints and of marrow, and [discerned] the thoughts and intentions of the heart" (Heb. 4:12). What's more, God's Word is described by Peter the Apostle as containing God's "precious and very great promises" (2 Peter 1:4). When believers take these promises and trust in them completely, their souls are nourished.[20]

Not only did your mom see God's Word as essential to nurturing her devotion to Jesus, she viewed prayer as being equally important. For her, prayer was simply talking to God, which included communicating her soul's desires to God as well as being the avenue of fellowship with Him.

She delighted in worshipping God, interceding for other people's needs like yours and mine. She also saw prayer as a tool to simply spend time with the one she loved the most–Jesus. The reason why your mom touched so many lives was because she knew God well. It was her greatest desire for you. She wanted you to know God like she knew God.

---

20 https://www.desiringgod.org/articles/gods-soul-food

The Bible says that parents are to train their children to know God's way, so when they become adults, they can be fruitful, godlily Christians. From day one, your mom and I had a plan for your spiritual growth.

Hugs and kisses,

Daddy

• • •

I Am Proud of You

Dear Faith,

The other day we were sitting on the couch and I asked you a question about what you thought your mom was doing right now. You said she was in heaven and was singing and dancing like a ballet mommy. You pictured her with Jesus laughing and have a great time.

Something else you said made my day. You said that mommy was proud of you. I am so glad that you still feel that way, even after a year. I see that her thumbprint on your life remains. You also could not have uttered a truer statement.

Before your mom passed away, we thought she had cancer, possibly even terminal. This fact weighed hard on your mom. She worried about dying and not being there for you anymore. The day before she died, she attended a service and shared her testimony about how God walked with her during her cancer scare. She again voiced her fear about leaving you alone without a mommy.

I must admit that I too was worried. Every little girl needs a mommy, just like every little girl needs a daddy. One reason why is that usually mommy's and daddy's parent a little differently. I know your mom and I did. I tended to be the disciplinarian, while your mom served as the nurturer. You needed to be exposed to both styles. You probably recognized that already.

When you were little, it was evident you were going to be a person who was tenacious and would not let a few failures get in your way. I remember taking you to the doctor when you were about 2 years old. You were just as cute then as you are now.

I was waiting for you to be seen by the doctor and you were playing next to another little girl. The little girl retrieved a book from the bookshelf and sat down on the small chair that sat next to the bookcase. As you sat there, you become intrigued. You wanted to do the same thing she was doing. It was evident that the wheels in your head were moving, trying to figure out how you were going to get in that chair.

After the nurse called the other girl's name, she and her mom made their way to the patient's room so they could be seen by the doctor. You decided to try your hand at sitting in the seat. You were determined to succeed.

I found out later that this level of determination to overcome any obstacle that stood in your way was part of who you were. This was evident when we got home and you tried to sit in the same kind of chair that was in our living room. You tried three or four times to climb on the chair, but again, to no avail. One more time you slipped and fell off the side of the chair resulting in a slightly bloody lip. I quickly attended to you by cleaning your wound and got you ready for supper. You were obviously frustrated when I asked you to come to the dinner table, as I had interrupted your pursuit to conquer the chair.

Mommy's motherly instinct took over when at dinner I told her what has happened at the doctor's office. She was concerned and was disappointed to hear what you went through.

When we finished dinner, your mom didn't want you to venture out again and try to mount another attempt to conquer the chair. I talked your mom into allowing you to try one more time.

She showed concern as she expressed sadness about your experience. After we finished eating, you made her way back to the living room. Your mom was a little hesitant to allow you to try to climb on the chair again. However, I persuaded her to let you try "one more time."

Then when Mommy saw you fall and hurt yourself, she wanted to wrap her arms around you and care for you. She wanted you to know that you were going to be safe.

Mommy's are the ones who take care of the bruises and mend the wounds. They are the ones who stay up with you when you are sick and teach you the facts of life when you are well. I love the quote by Washington Irving, who said, "A mother is the truest friend we have, when trials heavy and sudden, fall upon us; when adversity takes the place of prosperity; when friends who rejoice with us in our sunshine desert us; when trouble thickens around us, still will she cling to us, and endeavor by her kind precepts and counsels to dissipate the clouds of darkness, and cause peace to return to our hearts."[21] This describes your mommy very well.

Though your mom and I responded differently, I responded like a daddy and your mom responded like a mommy. We both were determined to allow you to discover your own limits. When we did, you finally made it onto that chair. You ended the evening conquering the chair.

Despite not having your mommy play the role in your life that she once did, it hasn't dissuaded you one bit. You have excelled at school, at church, and at home. You are still the same joy-filled little girl you have always been. Because of this, I am proud of you.

Hugs and kisses,

Daddy

---

21 https://www.goodreads.com/quotes/232474-a-mother-is-the-truest-friend-we-have-when-trials.

Thirteen

LETTERS OF ENCOURAGEMENT

Never Quit Smiling

Dear Faith,

One of the things I love about you is that you are a person who is happy almost all the time. You wake up happy, you go to school happy, and you come home happy. At your young age, you seem to have learned the secret of happiness.

The reason for your happiness is not your young age, however, because many kids your age aren't as happy as you. It is not because of your disability, because other kids with Down syndrome aren't as happy as you. You are just someone who has learned to enjoy life.

As I have watched you over the years, I think I have identified why you stay happy most of the time. G. K. Chesterton sums up your approach when he said, "When it comes to life the critical thing is whether you take things for granted or take them with gratitude."[22] Gratitude is a decision. We decide if we are going to

---

22 Quoted in https://www.goodreads.com/quotes/426236-when-it-comes-to-life-the-critical-thing-is-whether.

be grateful, because gratitude isn't dependent on circumstances. It is based upon your perspective and how you respond to your circumstances.

For you the glass is always half full instead of half empty. You have already learned to count your blessings. Even though you lost your mom, you have chosen not to focus on your loss, but to have an eternal perspective. You know that you will see your mom again. You have not lost her forever.

Just today, you climbed up onto my lap, like you used to when you were younger, and gave me a kiss. Then you talked about how much you look forward to seeing mommy one day. I saw in your eyes your sincerity. For you, this is not the power of positive thinking, but something you really believe.

You have taught me a lot about gratitude and happiness. Chesterton said that he learned more from watching children than he did out of any book. I concur. Since you joined our family, I have certainly learned a lot.

Your happiness and gratitude are illustrated through your smile. Your smile makes the world that much more beautiful. I see that smile every day when I pick you up in the car rider line. You wait until the teacher calls your name. Then when she does, you race out the door, with a beaming smile as if you can't wait to see me. This is one of the things I look forward to every day.

I must confess that sometimes I worry about you losing that smile one day. There are many adults who grew up with a beaming smile, only to lose it after enduring a traumatic experience.

I feared that for you when your mom died. You had a hard time with it at first. You weren't smiling as much, which was understandable. I'm thankful that you weren't shy about telling me when you were sad. There were more than a few times when you crawled in bed with me at night and wanted me to hold you because you were missing Mommy. We grieved her passing together.

You don't know how incredibly mature you were when doing this. You were facing your pain and wanting to talk about it, even though those conversations only lasted a few minutes. While you have developed a sense of gratitude, you will still need to learn patience in the future.

You still may have to go through some major losses in your life. It may be a loss of a friend or a loved one. Sometimes it is easier to get angry then to go through grieving. If this happens, please avoid that temptation. Don't let it take away your smile. You may be tempted one day to take life too seriously, or reflect on things you don't have. Avoid this and continue to learn the secret of being content. This will assure the smile will not leave you.

Hugs and kisses,

Daddy

• • •

Let's Maintain Our Relationship

Dear Faith,

I remember seeing you for the first time. You were just 12 hours old and so tiny. It didn't matter that you weren't my biological daughter, because the first moment I saw you, I fell in love with you. Since I never thought I would get the opportunity to have a daughter, I was so grateful to be a father to you, and I wanted to make the most of it.

When your mom used to walk by me as I was feeding you, she would say how obvious it was how you loved your daddy. This bond has grown even stronger since those early days.

The growth of our relationship has been intentional on my part because the relationship between a father and a daughter can have an amazing impact on a daughter for the rest of her life. God has designed all of us, including daughters, to need the nurturing and love of a father. Thus, a father needs to be committed to valuing and protecting his daughter and serve as an example of a dependable and responsible male. This requires that the father set aside time to talk, listen, and value his daughter. This is what I try to do for you.

I am intentional about setting aside time to spend with you. Therefore, I get up at 5 a.m. and start my day. I can get a few things done before you even wake up. Since we live less than five minutes away from school, I can drive you there. On most days, I can pick you up and then spend a couple hours with you until the caregiver arrives. I choose to spend the last three hours of the day working so I can spend time with you in the afternoon. This is a small sacrifice I am willing to make so I can spend time in the afternoon with the little girl I love so much.

One of the highlights of my day is when you and I sit down for a meal together. Sometimes we eat at home and sometimes we eat out. However, wherever we eat, the first words out of your mouth, even before we even sit down, are, "Daddy, I want some orange juice." I don't even remember when the orange juice obsession even got started, but it is difficult to get you to drink anything else. As you well know, I normally acquiesce to your wishes.

Of course, some of our meals together come with the extra bonus of entertainment. When we want to combine these two loves, we go to one of your favorite places on earth—Chuck E Cheese. Every time we drive into the parking lot, it is all I can do to get you to keep yourself buckled in until we park. Then when we enter the building, my next challenge is to keep you contained while I order our meal at the counter. When the food is ordered, and the tokens purchased, the real entertainment begins.

When I hand you your tokens, you first check and see if "Chucky" has come out to sing and dance with the other kids. If not, you race to play one of the video or arcade games or one of the other attractions. I, on the other hand, either follow you around and watch you play or participate in the playful atmosphere by stopping by to play Skeet-Ball or shoot hoops. Then when the food arrives, we both make a mad dash to enjoy some pizza and a soft drink. By the time we leave, both of us have thoroughly enjoyed ourselves.

The one activity that you thoroughly enjoy is when we just sit down and talk to one another. Since your daddy is a talker too, we get to do something that we both enjoy. You usually begin the conversation by asking me if I would like to talk. My response is always the same. Of course, I want to talk. You immediately reply by asking me what I want to talk about. Evidently, it is my job to always come up with the main topic of our conversation.

This brings me great joy, because as you grow older, normally daughters grow closer to their mothers and drift slowly away from the fathers. However, if our relationship that has been established early continues to be nurtured, it will blossom instead of succumbing to the temptation of growing apart.

It's a good sign that you have great conversational skills already, despite your young age. You ask good questions and genuinely care about what the other person has to say. Good listening shows that you truly care about the other person. These skills will continue to develop, and I look forward to helping you develop them.

I hope that when you get to be a teenager and beyond, you still will want to have these conversations. I hope to be one of the people you go to for advice. When you experience problems with a boyfriend or at work, feel free to pick up the phone and call Dad. Or, if you just want someone to hang out with, you know whom to contact. Maybe we can meet for lunch or a cup of coffee, just to talk about old times. Regardless, I am confident that our relationship will continue to blossom as you enter adulthood.

Hugs and kisses,

Daddy

• • •

Your Love of Reading

Dear Faith,

There is one thing that you love more than going to the park, coloring, or playing board games, and that is reading. A few years before you were born, your mommy began a master's degree in teaching reading. Many hours were spent studying, reading books, and writing papers. Sometimes having fun was set aside temporarily to finish her degree. Her rationale for getting the degree was to use it just in case the school system ever phased out Spanish, something the leadership in her district at the time was discussing as a possibility.

A few years after she graduated with that degree, we moved to Columbus, Indiana, which had a thriving Spanish program. She soon realized that there was much job security teaching Spanish in her new district. Therefore, she put the possibility of teaching reading to rest, assuming the reading degree would not be of any use.

When you came along, that all changed. From the very beginning, we read to you nearly every day, most of the time a minimum of an hour a day. A small part of me wondered if we should have spent our time doing something else, given your young age. Luckily, your mom's training and my previous training in elementary education informed us otherwise. Our education familiarized us with how children learn. We knew that a child's vocabulary grows exponentially if parents read to him or her early in life, which is why we committed to spend a certain amount of time every day reading to you.

Long before you were born, books were always a part of our home. Over the years the need to have a larger home was partly determined by the increasing number of books I was purchasing. Your mom was so happy when Amazon invented Kindle, so I could buy eBooks, which didn't take up any space.

Yet, despite growing up in such an atmosphere, your joy and love for reading seemed to be innate. Today, you would rather read a book than watch a television show or play a video game.

When you first began your love for reading, you were reading by yourself, though you didn't understand the words. I witnessed this for the first time one day as I was headed out the door and saw you out of the corner of my eye sitting in the middle of the family room reading to yourself. You were sitting in your chair, with your nose in your favorite book. I was so proud as the fruits of your mom's and my labor were made immediately visible to me that day.

The early years of reading to you nurtured a love of reading in you that complemented your God-given desire to read. When you were younger and didn't understand the words, your facial expressions told the story as you dramatized what you read.

About a year later, you began reading to your dolls. You would have three or four of them lined up side by side, reading to them the whole time. Obviously, you were a natural teacher as you mimicked your mom and me reading to you. You were extending that same commitment to teaching others to your dolls.

This is one of the blessings of parenthood, seeing you carry on in your mom's and my footsteps.

My goal was to have you reading on your own by the end of the first grade. You did not disappoint. One evening, as you were getting ready for bed, you asked to come back into the living room to join me. I handed you the book and asked you to read it to me. At first, you were reluctant. You politely asked me to read it to you. But I pressed this issue and had you read it. You read to me every word.

I never told you this, but after you went to bed, I went in my room because I was overcome by emotion, as this was something your mom didn't get to witness, but I did. You did it! You were reading on your own. We were told not to expect those kinds of results this early in your life. After all, you had a disability. However, we were determined not to place limits on you from the beginning. Instead, we wanted you to discover your own limits.

Over the years, reading has meant so much to me. I never was much of a reader until I was in my 20s. Then a whole new world was opened to me. I want that same thing to continue to happen to you.

Reading was also a big part of your mom's life. Her grandmother nurtured that desire in her. Your mom knew that God strategically placed her grandmother in her life to shape her into the person she became. She played an important role in your mom's life in many ways. Her love for reading opened a new world to your mom much earlier than it did me.

Several years ago, I read a story about a little girl like you who loved to read, and didn't value watching television quite as much. Her teacher was curious and asked her why. The little girl's response was priceless. She said she liked reading much better because the pictures were clearer. Reading helped to develop her imagination. G. K. Chesterton once said that imagination is the most important part of education. I think he is right!

It allows the words in a book instead of images on a television set to shape the mind.

I am so proud of you. You don't allow obstacles to stand in your way. You learned to read long before most people thought you would. As you grow older, continue not to allow me or anyone else put limits on you. Discover them for yourself. Then, when you do, don't beat yourself up about them. Just acknowledge that you are human, and all humans have limits.

Hugs and kisses,

Daddy

• • •

You Are Going to Make a Difference

Dear Faith,

Most people, while still being good, honest, and hardworking, make an average impact. They go about their lives just trying work hard, raise a family, and be good to others. Robert F. Kennedy, however, once said, "The purpose of life is to contribute in some way to making things better." Let me encourage you to contribute to make things better—which requires you to not settle for being average. Always strive to make a difference.

People who make a difference often share certain character traits. First, they have an inner fortitude that compels them to make a difference. They wake up every day with a purpose. They know they have been given a short time on earth and are determined to make the most of it. Someone else doesn't have to motivate them. They motivate themselves.

Second, like the first trait, people who make a difference are people of passion. They have an inner fire that doesn't go out. They get more excited about accomplishing things than the average person. There is an inner drive that sets them apart. I see this in you. You are not the type of person who needs someone to motivate her. It is just who you are.

When you know your purpose in life, it will fuel your passion. Roy T Bennet said, "If you have a strong purpose in life, you don't have to be pushed. Your passion will drive you there." Realize your purpose, never forget it, and then be fueled by it.

Third, they are optimistic. John Maxwell once said, "The difference between average people and achieving people is their perception of and response to failure." I believe this is so true. I have seen this in my own life. I have learned more from my failures than my successes.

I would add something else to Maxwell's statement. The difference between average people and achieving people is their perception and response to the challenges of life. We live in a fallen world. This means perfection does not come from the world we live in. You have already found out at an early age that the challenges that life brings can be overwhelming.

Fourth, people who make a difference are self-confident. You have no shortage of that trait. The advice Dr. Scully gave my mom when I was born—to not set limits for me but let me discover them—is still bearing fruit. This ethic was passed down to you, and you ran with it. You are one of the most optimistic people I know. You think you can do anything. But when you do find out your limitations, you are not crushed by it. You shrug it off and go on.

Finally, people who make a difference know how to connect with people. This is your best quality. Very few adults do it better than you do. Every time you walk into a room, you light it up. No matter where we travel, every time we walk into an airport, a restaurant, or a hotel people take notice of you and instantly fall in love. You have a way about you.

What endears people the most is how you love them. Touching people's hearts is how you win friends. It is how you impact lives. Even though you are only 8 years old, you have already made a tremendous difference in people's lives because you have touched their hearts.

You are one of those people born to make a difference. When you were just 3, a social justice class in one of the local high schools invited me to speak about raising a daughter with special needs. I asked if I could bring you and got an enthusiastic yes.

I watched you as you entered the room. You walked into the door with an inner confidence that permeated the room. In a room full of strangers, you were fearless. After I helped to remove your coat, you didn't need me anymore. You personally engaged with every student present by shaking his or her hand. Even though you were not able to say many words then, you didn't let that stop you.

What amazed me was the reaction of the students. Their eyes lit up, and it was obvious that they instantly fell in love with you. Like a politician who was campaigning for office, your smile, charisma, and warmth endeared you to everyone that day. They found you to be engaging, loving, and gracious. You did all of this without saying much. The genuineness that emanated from you instantly set you apart from everyone else. It was clear that you had what it takes to make a real and lasting difference in the lives of people. Your future is bright!

Hugs and kisses,

Daddy

• • •

Preparing for a New Mommy

Dear Faith,

Not too long ago you were getting ready for bed, going through our bedtime routine. It is always the same. First, you brush your teeth and then we pray. We begin by asking you what you would like me to pray for. This time you said you wanted me to pray that I get a wife and you get a mommy. It was obvious to me that this desire has been on your mind. It has been on my mind, too.

I have no idea when this will happen. It may be next year. It may not be until three years from now, or longer. There is a possibility it might not happen at all. However, I feel I need to prepare you just in case it does. Putting two families together comes with adjustments.

The best way to make the transition is for me and your new mommy to have a solid marriage. I promise to do what needs to be done to prepare to have a great marriage. The preparation before marriage and the friendship that is built before we walk down the aisle are key. I will do what I can to have a home that manifests love, respect, grace, and civility.

There will be some adjustments that you might have to make. I am very confident you will have no problems, but you should be aware how things might be different.

The first adjustment is where we might live. Depending on the new situation, we might need to move to a different house. If my new wife has kids, we will need a bigger house. My guess is that you will adjust just fine, but just in case it is a shock, I want to tell you beforehand.

Second, your new mommy will probably do things differently. After all, she is a different person. You remember when Mommy gave you a bath? It was a half-hour event. When Daddy gives you a bath, it lasts no more than five minutes. Why? Your mom and I are two different people, and we have two different ways of doing things.

A new mommy may do things differently, too. Maybe she is an indoor person like Daddy and really doesn't like things like camping. It will be an adjustment for you when you want to go camping in the backyard, because she might not want to. Then again, she might be very outdoorsy like Mommy was and love things like camping. If so, Daddy will need to make the adjustments.

Third, your new mommy might have kids. This will mean that you will have new brothers and sisters. You have been an only child for eight years. If you have brothers and sisters, it will take some getting used to. You might need to share a room. Or share toys. Or share time with Daddy with other kids. I am pretty sure you will do fine, but you need to know there will be adjustments.

Whatever the adjustments, I am confident everything will be okay. Remember, Daddy will always have your best interests at heart.

Hugs and kisses,

Daddy

Fourteen

LETTERS OF FATHERLY ADVICE

Uncle Shannon Dies

Dear Faith,

In an earlier letter, I talked about our coming Disney World trip, which will bring us fun times indeed. However, I regret to share with you some unfortunate news you probably won't fully understand.

Earlier today, I planned to meet Mike and Jody as well as Pastor Danny at the country club for lunch, then golf afterward. I was waiting for everyone to arrive, sipping a Diet Coke, when I received a phone call from your Uncle Josh. He told me your Uncle Shannon was killed. I couldn't believe my ears. I wasn't even sure how to process what I was hearing.

I regret that you are learning a lesson at such a young age that most people learn much later in life. Most parents hesitate to talk to their children about death because it is a very difficult subject. Had your mom and Uncle Shannon not passed away, I would have put off talking about the subject, too.

Unfortunately, all living things eventually die. You probably still remember Chip, our dog. You used to love to play with him, and he certainly loved you. Then a couple years ago we noticed him starting to get sick. He was a very old dog, so it was no surprise. You used to pet him when he was lying on the floor not feeling well. You asked me if he was going to get better, and I told you he probably wouldn't. Due to his age, I knew he didn't have much time left. As an older person, I knew that all living things die, but you were learning this for the first time. A week later, we put him to sleep.

Do you remember the memorial service we had for Chip? It lasted about 10 minutes. We talked about how much we loved him and briefly shared memories of him. Then I finished with a prayer. We did this because Chip had died and was never coming back.

Unfortunately, death is final. When people die, they don't come back to be with us. When your mom died, during the first few months you asked if Mommy was coming back. My reply was always the same. Your mommy was not coming back because she is in heaven.

You can rejoice that she is spending eternity there. You will see her one day. This is the hope of the resurrection of Jesus. Those who trust Him for their salvation will spend eternity in heaven. One day, you and your mom will be back together again. Except this time, you won't have to worry about ever being separated from her again. The Bible says that God will wipe away every tear from our eyes. That includes yours.

Despite having this eternal assurance to seeing believing loved ones again, we still have to face the challenge of being left behind to mourn their deaths. I am so proud of the way you have handled the tragedies you have experienced thus far. However, I know that you may have to deal with some issues surrounding your mom's death as you grow older. Right now, you might be too young to process everything, but one day you will. When that day arrives, I promise to be there to help walk you through each step.

Most importantly, let me encourage you to trust God. He loves you. He cares for you. He will listen to your cries and bring comfort to you. I come back to a certain Scripture again and again. It describes how Jesus wants us to come to Him with our burdens.

> *Come to me, all who labor and are heavy laden, and I will give you rest. Take my yoke upon you, and learn from me, for I am gentle and lowly in heart, and you will find rest for your souls. For my yoke is easy, and my burden is light." (Matt 11:28-30)*

Take comfort in the One who cares for you. He will never leave you or forsake you. Bring your cares, worries, hurts, and burdens to Him.

Love and kisses,

Daddy

• • •

Don't Get Bitter

Dear Faith,

I was sitting in the restaurant today when a thought crossed my mind. With all that has happened, I don't want you to become bitter. Right now, you are a bundle of joy. It has been a year now, and you have handled your mom's passing with incredible grace. Today, you are the opposite of bitter.

I wish I would have learned how to better handle adversity when I was younger. Most of the lessons I learned came later in life. Daddy was born with some deformities. My mom told me when I was a boy that her doctor gave her some medication that caused me to have a cleft palate, a cleft lip, and a webbed hand. I had to endure 20 operations, according to your grandma's count, and much ridicule from my peers. I had to learn to be tough quick.

My dad was a man you didn't ever get to meet, a man I didn't know well myself. He was an alcoholic. He would beat your grandma so often that she had to finally divorce him. Both experiences left me bitter.

I reacted by becoming an angry young man. I took to alcohol and drugs. By age 15, I was an alcoholic. From the time I was 15 years old until I was 21, I contemplated suicide daily. God had to get a hold of me and change me. This took some time.

You are 8 now. By the time you graduate high school, you will have celebrated 10 birthdays, 10 Easters, 10 Thanksgivings, and 10 Christmases. You will have gone through two metamorphoses, one called the teenage years, and the other, the beginning of adulthood. You will have had your first boyfriend, your first breakup, and your first kiss by then. Someone other than your mother will have to answer your questions about boys, breakups, and kisses. You won't receive the comfort of a mother's love, at least not the one you have known. All the experiences and special days I just mentioned will be spent without her.

Despite this, please know one thing. God loves you, and this world is not your final home. This is a truth you seem to know quite well already. Never forget it!

You are not just a pleasant child, but a tough one, too. I once went to visit you in preschool and observed you having lunch. While you were in the line, a boy kept trying to take your sandwich off your plate. Every one of his attempts was met with a slap on the hand by you. You were determined not to let the little boy push you around. It was clear to me that you were a tough cookie.

Then there was the time one of the boys from church said to you, about two weeks after your mom died, "You are the little girl whose mom died, right?" You didn't miss a beat. You told him that your name was Faith and your mommy was in heaven.

My prayer is that through the coming years you maintain this same line of thought. You are a living example of the advice given in the Book of James, when it says,

> Count it all joy ... when you meet trials of various kinds, for you know that the testing of your faith produces steadfastness. And let steadfastness have its full effect, that you may be perfect and complete, lacking in nothing. (James 1:2-4)

To count it all joy means to choose to respond in a certain way, despite the circumstances. Unfortunately, you don't choose your circumstances, but you do get to choose how you will respond to them.

This is where you have excelled thus far. My prayer is that you will continue to respond the same way when you experience the tough times ahead. When you do, remember the words from Habakkuk, who said,

> God, the Lord, is my strength; he makes my feet like the deer's; he makes me tread on my high places. To the choirmaster: with stringed instruments. (Hab. 3:9)

In the coming years, continue to allow God to be your strength. Look to Him for guidance. Cry out to Him for comfort when you experience things you don't understand.

My vision for you is one of success. I have no reason to think otherwise. As I ponder the possibilities of your future, I see a beautiful young woman walking down the aisle getting married, all the while smiling with that incredible smile of yours, waving at your daddy.

I will be looking on, probably with tears flowing down my face, because I will know all the things you have gone through and the tragedy you have had to endure. Instead of bitterness, your life will reflect the advice once given by the prophet Isaiah, who said "to give them a beautiful headdress instead of ashes, the oil of gladness instead of mourning, the garment of praise instead of a faint spirit; that they may be called oaks of righteousness, the planting of the Lord, that he may be glorified." You will be this woman who walks down that aisle.

Somehow, I expect to see a part of your mom in you that day. The part that was gracious, who loved to smile, and beaming with both inner and outer beauty. There will be a piece of her that is still alive and well, because her ministry to you those first six years will continue to be lived out in your life.

Her hand prints will be evident. I look forward to that day.

Hugs and kisses,

Daddy

• • •

Going Out to Eat

Dear Faith,

One of the things your mom and I used to love to do was go out to eat. Before we had you, we did it frequently. Luckily, we liked the same kinds of food, so it made our choice about where to eat an easy one.

There is one time I will never forget. I took your mom to Indianapolis for her birthday. We began the evening watching a movie at the IMAX theater. She loved the IMAX.

After the movie, we went to dinner. I wasn't sure where we would go, but we happened to drive by a Brazilian steakhouse. This was my first such experience. At the time, the atmosphere was a bit fancier that I was used to, but I have adapted since then.

The salad bar was unlike anything I had ever seen. I needed labels to identify most of the food. Eating there was going to be a culinary adventure for me.

Your mom and I were seated, and soon we began to enjoy our meal. They brought out the food in courses. I couldn't wait to begin eating the Brazilian-style meat. Right before they brought us the first round of steak, I embarrassed your mom by asking the waiter for ketchup. I couldn't fathom eating meat without it. Your mom was beside herself. I am not sure why it took her by surprise. We had been married a long time by them, and I had been eating steak the same way during our entire marriage. Maybe she thought the elegant atmosphere was going to restrain me from giving in to my redneck tendencies.

When you came along, things changed. We wanted to eat at home more. Your mom and I both had fond memories of conversations at the dinner table when we were growing up. This was before iPad, iPhone, and laptop computers. The only distraction available at that time was TV, and if you didn't have cable, the only thing on TV was the news. News was a lot different then. No yelling, screaming, or name-calling. It was just news.

Talking to one another served as our entertainment when I was a boy. The topic most often discussed was what we did that day. I usually hesitated because I often got into trouble at school. If I got into trouble that day and the principal failed to call my home, why did I need to do his job and tell my mom at the dinner table? I tried to either keep quiet or make up a story.

Your mom and I wanted to recapture part of our childhood by dining together at home every night. Therefore, we passed by all the restaurants on the way after school and either Daddy or Mommy began to fix supper.

The dinner table is where we learn how to pray before every meal, talk about how our days went, and get to know one another a little better every day.

But when your mom passed away, things changed. A couple weeks after she passed, you and I were eating supper at the kitchen table. Except that day I didn't talk much. As we were eating, my eyes wandered to stare at the empty chair where your mom once sat. It took me nearly a year to figure out why we ate out so much. Nearly every meal was spent eating at a restaurant because at home I had to look at the empty chair, which reminded me that your mom was no longer with us.

I have decided to cut back on dining out. Instead, I am going to begin cooking again so we can eat at home. I hope to make new memories around our dinner table. So I will need to learn how to cook healthy meals. You and I have gotten used to going to restaurants where they serve healthy meals. What those restaurants can't do is recreate the home atmosphere needed to have conversations that bond a family together.

Hugs and kisses,

Daddy

• • •

What it Means to Be a Woman

Dear Faith,

Since your mom is in heaven and is no longer with us, it is up to me, a man and your daddy, to teach you what it means to be a woman. This is a formable task because both society and the church are very confused about the roles of men and women.

The problem is that our secular culture overemphasizes equality and minimizes the differences between men and women. Yet the Bible teaches us that men and women are equal but are to relate to one another in complementary ways. God has designed the family to include a husband and wife and a mother and father.

One of the roles the mother plays is to teach her kids what it means to be a woman. Femininity should be first learned at home. For example, the mom teaches her children how to relate to the opposite sex.

She also models what it means to be a mom. The mom serves multiple roles, such as supporting her husband, nurturing the spiritual lives of her children, valuing each child in the different ways that God has made them, encouraging them, disciplining them, and instructing them to be people who love God and follow His ways.

One of your mom's greatest desires was to teach you how to be a woman. Since she is not here to teach you, I will explain a little bit about her, so her example can still make an impact on you. She would have been the perfect person to teach you about being a wife. If you want to know how a woman relates to her husband, your mom is a perfect example.

She loved me a lot and was always willing to sacrifice for me and me for her. Often she put my needs before her own. When I felt called to plant a church in East Chicago, Indiana, a very rough place to pastor and live, she happily quit her job and followed me there. When I felt God call me to pastor a small church in Bloomfield, Indiana, she willingly resigned her job and followed me there. God has rewarded her faithfulness. Each time she quit her job for ministry, God gave her a better-paying job in better circumstances.

Not only did she move there with me, she partnered with me in ministry and fulfilled key roles in the church. She saw herself as a helpmate to me. Many women would have never made the sacrifices that your mom made for me in ministry. These are only a couple of examples of her love and sacrifice. During our 23 years of marriage, I witnessed many more.

She is a great role model for motherhood, too. When your mother came home from a hard day's work, she still made time to spend a couple hours every day with you. After dinner, you had her full attention until it was time for bed. This was her favorite time of the day. She read to you, helped you with your homework, gave you a bath and put you to bed. Then when you were in bed, she spent an hour or two preparing to teach the next day. She was one of a kind.

Like Daddy, Mommy wanted to develop a strong bond with you. Therefore, she always took you to the park. It was something you both liked to do together.

There is one role the mother plays that doesn't end when the child leaves the home, and that is as a confidant. She wanted to be the one you went to when you needed advice. Now, you will have to lean on someone else. Maybe me, maybe a relative, or maybe even a friend. If these types of relationships take time to develop, make sure you take that time to develop them. Since your mom is no longer with us, you might be tempted to go it alone. Resist that temptation when it comes.

Hugs and kisses,

Daddy

• • •

You Will Be a Strong Woman

Dear Faith,

Let me begin by saying I think you are going to be a strong woman. However, there are differing ideas about what "strong woman" means, so let's define this concept.

When secular people use the term, they are focusing primarily on asserting one's independence. I read an article by Danielle

Campoamor in the Huffington Post about what she thinks is a strong woman.

Campoamor recounts the evolution of her understanding of the term. When she was in elementary school, being a strong woman meant getting picked first for the kickball team. In middle school, she thought she needed to continue to have certain sports aspirations, such as playing basketball and volleyball. But she included other things such as "choosing Shop instead of Home Ec, and saying 'no' to boys when so many of [her] friends were starting to say 'yes.' When she moved on to high school, she thought being a strong woman meant going shot-for-shot [drinking] with [her] male friends."[23]

Finally, in college, she "thought it meant experimenting sexually and with conscious fluidity." She "was told it meant refusing to shave [her] armpits or legs, if only to fight a patriarchal society's view of femininity." She "was convinced it meant fighting back against the social pressure to get married and have children."[24]

When she became an adult, her perception changed once more. She believed that being a strong woman meant "being unapologetically, fiercely and wholeheartedly *you*."[25] The article goes on to detail her version of a strong woman. Yet her version knows nothing of strength; only selfishness. For her a strong woman meant putting your child up for adoption, having an abortion, dressing immodestly, being arrogant, and refusing to be gracious. In other words, being a strong woman means building your life solely around yourself.

This version of a strong woman is a cheap counterfeit to what a strong woman really is. Your mommy was a strong, successful

---

23 Danielle Campoamore, "What It Means to Be a 'Strong Woman,'" *HuffPost*, updated October 21, 2016, https://www.huffingtonpost.com/danielle-campoamor/what-it-means-to-be-a-strong-woman_b_8341406.html, accessed November 7, 2017.
24 Ibid.
25 Ibid.

woman. But her paradigm didn't come from Gloria Steinem or Simone de Beauvoir, who were secular feminist thinkers. It came from Proverbs 31.

This version is not popular. You and I live in an age of what some call "radical individualism" or what one writer called "expressive individualism."[26] This type of individualism "holds that society should create space for and celebrate the free expression of an individual's natural desires and inclinations."[27] This is the value system expressed in the article I just mentioned.

However, my prayer is that you adopt another model that "holds that the natural inclinations of the self should at times be forsaken in service of a divine purpose, and that social and moral tradition can appropriately encourage such values."[28] The Proverbs 31 model is a great guide.

This model begins with servanthood. The theme of servanthood was also modeled by Jesus. One time, Jesus witnessed his disciples arguing about who would be the greatest among them. He interjected a principle that they had never heard. People of the time thought that being great meant lording over people, getting your own way, furthering your own agenda, and seeking personal fulfillment above everyone else. He countered by teaching that whoever aspires to be great must be a servant. Jesus finished by offering Himself as a role model, stating that the "Son of Man came not to be served but to serve, and to give his life as a ransom for many" (Matt. 20:25-28).

---

26 Robert N. Bellah, Richard Madsen, William M. Sullivan Ann Swidler, Steven M. Tipton, *Habits of the Heart: Individualism and Commitment in American Life* (Oakland, Calif.: University of California Press, 2007), Kindle Location 74.

27 Quoted in https://discussingmarriage.org/expressive-individualism-vs-christian-discipleship/#.Wd6NQztrzIU, accessed November 7, 2017.

28 Ibid.

From Proverbs 31, we gather that a strong woman means, first of all, being an excellent wife. This does not mean you must get married, but it does mean that if you do, use this as an opportunity to serve your family. The husband is also called to do the same.

Your mom was a great example. She came home after working all day as a teacher, then loved you enough that she spent at least two hours with you before you went to bed. She colored with you, played games with you, gave you a bath, and helped you clean your room. She sacrificed because she loved you.

When you went to bed, she finished the evening by doing school work and even spent the last hour with your daddy. It was easy to sacrifice for her. Proverbs 31 captures how I felt about your mommy. It states, "The heart of her husband trusts in her, and he will have no lack of gain. She does him good, and not harm, all the days of her life" (Prov. 31:11-12).

Proverbs 31 also says that the strong woman takes care of her family's needs. But she doesn't have to be secluded at home. The woman in this chapter was successful outside the home by making business deals and earning money. She got up early and stayed up late. She refused "to eat the bread of idleness." She also cared about the needs of the poor. She taught kindness and exuded grace in her actions.

What is particularly nice is that her husband and children responded to her by giving the credit and accolades she deserved.

The most important characteristic of a strong woman is that she is not proudly independent and self-reliant or even charming and beautiful, because "charm is deceitful, and beauty is vain" (Prov. 31:30). Instead, what is most important is that she is "a woman who fears the LORD" (PROV. 31:10). So she will be recognized for the person she is, as "her works praise her in the gates" (Prov. 31:31).

Hugs and kisses,

Daddy

• • •

We Need to Make New Memories

Dear Faith,

I have been thinking a lot lately about our need to make new memories. There are always seasons in life during which things change. Growing up we had Thanksgiving and Christmas rituals that we did every year. On Thanksgiving, my mom fixed baked beans, deviled eggs, sweet potatoes, and turkey. After lunch, we all went to the living room to watch the early NFL game.

After that game was over, I went over to my cousin Jeff's house to watch the evening game, play cards, and eat leftovers from their Thanksgiving feast. I still remember my Uncle Bill cracking us all up. Those were great times.

Christmas morning was spent opening presents. I was always the first one to wake up, usually around 4:00 or 5:00 in the morning, which made me a popular guy! I felt it was my job to wake everyone else and let them know that Santa had arrived. I remember being so excited I could hardly sleep.

One Christmas, your Uncle Shannon and I got Evel Knievel bikes for Christmas. We had to wait three months until it was warm enough to ride them outside. When the moment of truth arrived, and Mom let us take them outside, I encouraged my brother to jump off the porch with his bike. He resisted at first, but I convinced him that he wouldn't get hurt because he was riding an Evel Knievel bike. He took the bait and the rest is history. He jumped off the porch and went headfirst over the handlebars. This was followed by a blood-curdling scream that I think even the neighbors heard. My mom rushed out to see what the matter was and tended to his scraped chin. Once he was okay, she tended to my backside!

When I married your mother, we made new memories. While growing up, she celebrated the holiday on Christmas Eve. I celebrated it on Christmas Day. When we got married, we began a new tradition. We enjoyed a nice Christmas Eve candlelight dinner, just the two of us. After dinner, we went to the couch, where I read the Christmas story. Then we each opened a present. My favorite part of the evening came next. Your mom and I sat next to each on the couch and watched a Christmas movie.

Then you came along. Now your mom and I could make new memories. The one that stands out the most for me was Christmas Day. After you were born, the excitement I had as a child reemerged because I couldn't wait for you to wake up and open your presents. You were the most excited person on the planet. Your mom recorded you opening presents every year. Not only did we see your excitement, but others were able share in it through social media.

Your mommy has passed away, but you and I will make new memories together. Last Thanksgiving and Christmas was just us. For Thanksgiving, we went to Disney. This probably won't be a yearly ritual. My guess is that we will go to my grandma's house for Thanksgiving. For Christmas, we will go to Christmas Eve service then home to open a present in honor of Mommy. After that, we will carry on her tradition of reading the Christmas story. Next morning we will open presents, then go to my mom's house for Christmas dinner. The next day I will drive you to Michigan so you can spend a week with your Aunt Roberta. These will be our new traditions.

I do want to tell you that the traditions might change if I remarry. I am not sure what they will be, but I know that they will be fun and you will be there by my side. We will have a great future together.

Hugs and kisses,

Daddy

Fifteen

Dear Michelle,

I remember the day I asked you to marry me. We walked to the park near my grandmother's house, where we spent so much time together. When we arrived, we sat at the picnic table where we had so many rich conversations.

Nervous, I wondered if you were going to say *yes* to my proposal. It was a cool autumn night, but I was sweating from anxiety.

As I reached into my pocket and knelt on one knee, the moment of truth had arrived. I mustered all the confidence I could and asked, "Will you marry me?" Your response was priceless: "I guess." While I took that as a reluctant *yes*, it was good enough for me. You confirmed that you wanted to be my wife.

It would be 10 months until you and I would walk down the aisle and become husband and wife. Mark 10:7 reads, "'Therefore a man shall leave his father and mother and hold fast to his wife and the two shall become one flesh." When I studied this verse before we were married, I discovered that all my relationship loyalties would need to be subservient to my relationship with you, which meant that my heart was to be devoted to you as my primary human relationship.

The day we said our vows, we became one flesh, which meant we would share life together by having "one life, one reputation, one bed, one suffering, one budget, one family, one mission, and so forth. No barriers. No hiding. No aloofness. Now total openness with total sharing and total solidarity, until death parts them."[29] We grew together as husband and wife. I want to thank you for the 23 wonderful years we had together. I will never forget them.

Over those years, the way you loved me, the patience you showed me, the care you extended to me all made me the man I am today.

When we married, I had just been saved for about four years and was still pretty jaded and needed to grow spiritually. I was plagued by a very low sense of self-worth and fear along with an anxiety that made life almost unbearable at times. For years, it was tough for me to be in crowds or to handle rejection at work, which many people today would find hard to believe.

You saw in me things I never saw in myself. You were always the one who encouraged me when I felt I wasn't good enough to complete the task. You saw not just what I was but what I could be. I latched onto your vision because it inspired me to strive for new heights.

Some of my favorite moments in our marriage were the times we prayed together at night. We made it nearly a nightly ritual, spending the last 10 minutes of our evening praying for one another's requests.

Your prayers at night were particularly impactful. Many times, when you prayed it was like God had given you direct spiritual

---

29 Ray Ortlund, "What is marriage, according to the Bible?" The Gospel Coalition, June 26, 2015, https://blogs.thegospelcoalition.org/rayortlund/2015/06/26/what-is-marriage-according-to-the-bible/, accessed November 7, 2017.

insight into my situation. On multiple occasions, the impact of your prayers was felt immediately. Your petitions were always timely, your words were always soothing, and your care and love always obvious.

It was during this prayer time that God moved in life-changing ways for me. My battle with rejection and fear was overcome as you fought the spiritual battle with me.

Another reason I am grateful for you is the unconditional love you showed me. When I came to our marriage, I didn't fully understand God's love. The years of rejection I received made it difficult to see how anyone could love me, especially God. Yet God used you to teach me His unconditional love and grace. I couldn't grasp them fully until I experienced them in a tangible way through you.

In many ways, I am a product of your ministry as my wife. You always took that role seriously and lived it out so wonderfully. You were a helpmate to me. You offered advice and encouraged me when I became discouraged.

For the last six years of your life you were able to experience what your heart longed for all your life, which was to be a mother. You were the best. You took your job seriously. This was a role that you were destined to play.

You served Faith sacrificially just as you did me. The day you died, you were not feeling well. Yet despite your feelings, you took Faith to the park. This was a fitting way to end your time on earth. You could share one last special moment with the daughter you loved. Going to the park was something you two used to love to do together. Faith still talks about the fun she had.

Not long ago I asked Faith what Mommy was now doing since she was in heaven. Her response was priceless. She said you were singing and dancing. Then her face lit up as if she caught a glimpse of what you were enjoying in heaven.

Then she revealed the impact you made in her. She said, "Mommy is proud of me." This was made possible because for you, the glass was always half-full instead of half-empty. You didn't set limitations for Faith. You allowed her to discover the limitations on her own. You had a knack for nurturing her special interests. Things like coloring, painting, and reading were things she loved to do. You coached her in how to do those things better and praised her when she did. These things instilled in her the assurance that her mom was proud of her. As a result, she will accomplish so much more in life because you took time to pour into her.

It has been over a year since you passed away, and I have a void that I have been praying to be filled. I no longer have a helpmate to walk beside me, and Faith no longer has a mother to love her unconditionally and pour into her.

When you were going through the cancer scare, we talked about what I should do if you were to pass away. You strongly encouraged me to find someone else. I now have followed your advice and entered the world of dating, and what a world it is. People no longer meet at church or even in their hometown, for that matter. They meet online. You read bios and send smiles. The method is very shallow and consumer-driven. I am trusting God to put me together with the right one. I refuse to settle for second best.

This is very difficult for me to do since I loved you so much, but I am writing to say goodbye. I want to thank you again for the 23 wonderful years we spent together and the impact you made in my life. We were truly one flesh, as I already mentioned. Yet this connection must be severed so I can find someone with whom I can build that same bond.

As I search for a wife, I do so with Faith in mind. We are a package deal. The woman I marry must love Faith as if she is her own and love Jesus with all her heart. This person is out there somewhere. I just need to find her. I am trusting God to lead me to her. He gave me you. After all, you asked me out the first time. You made it easy for me. Maybe it will be that way again. Whatever the case, I look forward to seeing you one day in eternity where we will all be together again.

Love,

Tim

Sixteen

FINAL THOUGHTS

My life is not what I would have chosen, but it is the life I was given. I have learned to thank God every day for it. Through my personal sufferings, I have learned that God's grace in Christ is sufficient for me because it has taught me to depend on Him.

The Apostle Paul learned the same lesson when he asked cried out to God to remove the thorn in his flesh. The Lord answered Paul's cry: "My grace is sufficient for you, for my power is made perfect in weakness" (2 Cor. 12:9b). What exactly, as modern readers, are we to make of this incredibly countercultural statement? It is this: God's grace not only saves us but also sustains us.[30] Paul was acquainted with great suffering, yet the Lord sustained him.

No doubt Paul's resume of suffering was unmatched. It included hard labor, imprisonment, and beatings that nearly killed him. He was stoned, shipwrecked, and in danger. He endured sleepless nights and torrential weather. He faced anxieties that stemmed from his ministry responsibilities. Yet you don't see a pity party from Paul. There is no

---

30 David Garland, *2 Corinthians: An Exegetical and Theological Exposition of Holy Scripture* (Nashville: Holman Reference, 1999), Kindle Locations 12922-12923.

"poor me" language in anything he wrote. Instead, he chose to boast in his affliction. How many us of would have responded that way?

Paul rejoiced in his affliction because of the spiritual fruit it produced. He states, "Therefore I will boast all the more gladly of my weaknesses, so that the power of Christ may rest upon me. For the sake of Christ, then, I am content with weaknesses, insults, hardships, persecutions, and calamities. For when I am weak, then I am strong" (2 Cor. 12:9c-10).

Hardships forced Paul to draw on Christ's strength. By receiving the revelations he did, he was in danger of succumbing to pride. Thus, God allowed him to be made "acutely aware of his own inadequacies and prevents him from thinking that he is equal to the task alone. It prevents a bloated ego from crowding out the power of God in his life. Paul now reveals why he is so willing to boast in his weakness rather than to pray for its removal."[31] Who hasn't seen talented men and women attempt to do God's work by operating in their own strength? God sometimes allows suffering to help curb that tendency.

However, how one responds to the suffering is key. For some, suffering produces anger and bitterness. For others, suffering makes them more like Christ. One's response determines what suffering will do to the person. I will resist the temptation to offer examples of men and women who failed the test. Yet Paul passed it. Why? "If Paul boasted in his own strength, thinking that by himself he was equal to any task or any calamity, he would then cancel out the power of God in his life. [He understood that] [h]e is therefore most powerful when he is least reliant on his own resources."[32] Dependence on God was the source of his boasting.

A Final Word

I hope I have communicated how God can work out all things for our good, even in the face of tragedy. Despite growing up with multiple birth defects and enduring a broken and abusive home life, having

---

31 Garland, Kindle Locations 12934-12936.
32 Garland, Kindle Locations 12948-12950.

my daughter witness my wife's death, and—if all that wasn't enough—shortly thereafter hearing of my brother's violent death, I clung to God's promise that hope exists beyond this world. Such hope can lead to our happiness despite life's difficult circumstances, as we learn to depend on God, even in the face of suffering.

We live in a broken world. At the beginning, mankind enjoyed complete and unobstructed fellowship with God. There was no brokenness. Then, because of the sin of Adam and Eve, the first human beings, sin came into the world, and fellowship and the intimate connection with God were lost. "One of the tragic implications of this event is that man lost his secure status with God and began to struggle with feelings of arrogance, inadequacy, and despair, valuing the opinions of others more than the truth of God. This robbed man of his true self-worth and put him on a continual, but fruitless, search for significance," security, and peace.[33] Sin results in men and women who are broken.

When something is broken, we usually throw it away. Whenever I break a dish, I don't try to glue it together so I can eat off of it again. Why? Because it is no longer useful to me. Fortunately, with God, the opposite is true with His children. God sees people as broken vessels who need to be mended and restored.[34] Scripture teaches that "the Lord is close to the brokenhearted" (Psalm 34:18). God is the loving heavenly Father who acts as a Shepherd to His people.

His methods of fixing brokenness, however, may not be to our liking. As a matter of fact, His methods may not be what we think a loving heavenly Father would use to heal His child's brokenness. Secular-minded people are aghast that God sometimes uses suffering to do it. When He does, it is as a loving Shepherd. The image of a shepherd helps us to understand God's loving care for us during suffering.

---

33 Robert McGee, *The Search for Significance: Seeing Your True Worth Through God's Eyes* (Nashville: Thomas Nelson, 2003), Kindle Locations 419-422.

34 Quoted in https://www.gotquestions.org/Bible-brokenness.html.

The shepherd's job is to care for the sheep. He is charged with tending, guarding, and caring for the sheep. He always has the sheep's best interests at heart.

God's ministry of shepherding is reflected in Psalm 23. God is pictured as a protector and a provider for sheep who need care. The analogy is not meant to be flattering to us, however. Sheep are helpless creatures that need someone to care for them. If left alone, they will actually harm themselves. They are dumb animals that need someone to protect and care for them.

People are like sheep. They too are dependent and need care. People naturally wander from the shepherd. They want to be independent but are not capable of doing well on their own. They think dependence on the shepherd is not needed. In extreme circumstances, the shepherd will break the legs of the sheep and place it on the back of his neck. The goal is to teach the sheep to depend on the shepherd. This is what God did with me. By living through the deaths of my wife and brother, my legs were broken, and I was forced to depend on the shepherd.

Some may ask a valid question at this point: Are you saying that God allowed Michelle and Shannon to die to teach you this valuable lesson? My answer is no. After all, He had many other ways at his disposal to teach me the lesson. I believe that before people are born, God assigns them a certain amount of days on this earth. Michelle and Shannon's times were up. God simply took the opportunity to use their deaths to serve other purposes. One purpose was to conform me more completely into the image of His Son.

To be sure, sometimes God allows difficult circumstances so we will be broken and depend on the Shepherd. When those circumstances come, it is important to know that God is the Good Shepherd who cares for His sheep, protects His sheep, feeds His sheep, and works on their behalf, especially in the hard times.

Since Michelle passed away, I have learned valuable lessons and experienced incredible life transformation, as God has been a Good Shepherd to me. When tragedy happens, you must go to your source of comfort, stability, and strength. Tragedy caused me to grow deeper in my relationship with God.

The Protestant Reformer Martin Luther had something to say about suffering and how it heals our brokenness. The *New York Times* bestselling author Tim Keller offers solid commentary on Luther's understanding.

> In Luther's view, suffering plays a dual role. Before we get the joy and love that help us to face and overcome suffering, suffering must first empty us of our pride and lead us to find our true joy and only security in Christ. Luther declares, "For since God takes away all our goods and our life through many tribulations, it is impossible for the heart to be calm and to bear this unless it clings to better goods, that is, united with God through faith." Suffering dispels the illusion that we have the strength and competence to rule our own lives and save ourselves. People "become nothing through suffering" so that they can be filled with God and his grace.[35]

For Luther, suffering paves the way for a deeper relationship with God because it empties us of our own self-sufficiency. We are compelled to rely on God as our source. Therefore, James said to "count it all joy … when you meet trials of various kinds, for you know that the testing of your faith produces steadfastness. And let steadfastness have its full effect, that you may be perfect and complete, lacking in nothing" (James 1:2-4). Thus, Christians can rejoice through suffering because of the spiritual fruit it produces.

To live out this command given by James requires a deep understanding of the sovereignty and goodness of God. The sovereignty of God says that God is absolutely in control of everything that happens in the universe. His rule extends over all of creation. Nothing happens that He doesn't allow. Therefore, God might not be the *cause* of all suffering, but He is the One who *allows* it. Since God is sovereign, I can rejoice

---

35 Keller, Kindle Locations 829-833.

during my suffering because there will be a limit to it. This realization brought me great comfort during very difficult times. I knew that God was managing what was happening for my good.

The goodness of God, on the other hand, says that everything God does is good, because everything He does emanates from His nature, which is wholly good. Returning to James, we read, "Every good gift and every perfect gift is from above, coming down from the Father of lights, with whom there is no variation or shadow due to change" (James 1:17).

What James is saying is that "God is the final understanding of good, and that all that God is and does is worthy of approval."[36] Thus, the idea of God's sovereignty and goodness is what helps makes sense of Paul's articulation of God's plan for suffering when he said, "And we know that for those who love God all things work together for good, for those who are called according to his purpose" (Rom. 8:28). When we suffer, we are comforted to know that God is in control of everything that happens and has our best interest at heart.

I think I have been given a glimpse how God used the tragedies I experienced for His glory. When Michelle died, I needed answers, so I scoured the internet for them. During my search, I found a series of lectures at Oxford University delivered by Tim Keller to be incredibly helpful.

Keller's premise was that everyone needs meaning, satisfaction, freedom, identity, and hope. Later I stumbled onto his book *Making Sense of God: An Invitation to the Skeptical* that was also helpful. (I have quoted it several times in this book.) These tragedies caused me to turn to the ultimate One who supplied me with the answers to my heart longings. And in a deeper way, Jesus became an even greater source of my meaning, satisfaction, freedom, identity, and hope. Let me share how that worked out in my own experience.

---

36 Wayne Grudem, *Systemic Theology: An Introduction to Biblical Doctrine* (Grand Rapids, Zondervan Publishing House, 1994), 197.

Meaning

The first thing I needed to locate was meaning. Human beings are the only creatures in the world to search for meaning, because they are the only beings who have that capacity. Sociologists of religion hypothesize that most of the world is religious because human beings ask such existential questions, and religion is where most people find these answers.

Therefore, the quest for meaning is a universal phenomenon, and multiple answers are given in our world about how to find it. Secular people, such as the writer and mythologist Joseph Campbell, express their understanding of meaning in fatalistic terms. Campbell said, "Life has no meaning. Each of us has meaning and we bring it to life. It is a waste to be asking the question when you are the answer."[37] For Campbell, life has no inherent meaning. Meaning is not discoverable, because without God, there can be no essential meaning in the universe. Meaning must be manufactured. If Campbell is correct, when human beings speak of meaning, they are simply uttering the useful fiction they have created to get them through life. I couldn't disagree more.

Because God supplies the overall purpose for our lives and gives us duties to fulfill, meaning begins with Him. The Christian story speaks of a loving God who created us so we can know Him. However, Adam and Eve sinned, creating a chasm separating all of us from God. Christ's death and resurrection, however, allow men and women to be reconciled to God and one day to spend eternity with Him in heaven. My relationship with Him and the eternal destiny that awaits me supply me with ultimate meaning. Unlike Joseph Campbell, I didn't have to manufacture meaning. I already possess it.

The concept of meaning serves two functions, offering us both purpose and significance. "So, to have meaning in life is to have both an overall purpose for living and the assurance that you are making a difference by serving some good beyond yourself."[38] In my newfound posi-

---

37 Quoted in https://www.goodreads.com/quotes/178306-life-has-no-meaning-each-of-us-has-meaning-and.

38 Keller, 58.

tion as a Christian, I was forced to ask myself what brought me ultimate purpose and what difference I was called to make.

In contrast, if my marriage was what gave me ultimate meaning and purpose in life, then Michelle's death would have made my life meaningless. I was already convinced intellectually that meaning came from my relationship with God, but I knew I needed to reexamine where I was placing my trust. To find comfort, I turned to Scripture. It reminded me of the type of relationship Jesus wanted with me. As I struggled with my loss, I was reminded that God supplied me with ultimate meaning. If my relationship with God was my ultimate source of meaning, then it could not be taken away—because it lay outside this world. Paradoxically, since meaning for me "is to know, please, emulate, and be with God, then [my] suffering ... enhance[d] meaning in [my] life, because it" drew me "closer to him,"[39] I looked more deeply into how I am to relate with God.

Part of what God offers through Christ is friendship, a fact that surprises a lot of people. Jesus declared to his disciples, "No longer do I call you servants, for the servant does not know what his master is doing; but I have called you friends, for all that I have heard from my Father I have made known to you" (John 15:15). Literally, we can be friends with God.

Such a proposition, however, is absurd to many people. How do Christians understand this apparent "absurdity"? First, we need to grasp that God initiates the friendship, not us. He "has befriended us in Christ."[40] Through this friendship, we are called to enjoy and deepen our relationship with Him.

To understand the conditions of that relationship, one needs to understand the terms of that friendship. Don Carson offers a great perspective: "Mutual, reciprocal friendship of the modern variety is not in view, and cannot be without demeaning God."[41] He is still Lord and we are still his servants. He invites us into the friendship on that basis.

---

39 Keller, 73.

40 Quoted in Aaron Menikoff, "The Gospel and Friendship," September 18, 2009, The Gospel Coalition, *https://www.thegospelcoalition.org/article/the-gospel-and-friendship-part-i*, accessed November 9, 2017.

41 Ibid.

The hymn titled *What a Friend We Have in Jesus* by Joseph Scriven captures this idea quite well and was the one that I turned to in my hour of need. It says:

> What a friend we have in Jesus,
> All our sins and griefs to bear!
> What a privilege to carry
> Everything to God in prayer!
> Oh, what peace we often forfeit,
> Oh, what needless pain we bear,
> All because we do not carry
> Everything to God in prayer!

The first verse expresses the kind of relationship Jesus wants. It reminded me that I have a friend in Jesus. This is part of what brings me meaning. After the hymn opens by citing this truth, it explains that the foundation for our friendship is based on what Jesus did to establish it: "All our sins and griefs to bear." Jesus paid the ultimate price to establish this friendship. He provided the atonement needed to reconcile me to God. Because of this reconciliation, I could take my burdens and give them to Him.

To be sure, I had a choice about whether I would bear this burden myself, as the above verse mentions, or take it to God in prayer. By His grace, I chose the latter, as the next verses exhort us to do.

> Have we trials and temptations?
> Is there trouble anywhere?
> We should never be discouraged—
> Take it to the Lord in prayer.
> Can we find a friend so faithful,
> Who will all our sorrows share?
> Jesus knows our every weakness;
> Take it to the Lord in prayer.

Are we weak and heavy-laden,
Cumbered with a load of care?
Precious Savior, still our refuge—
Take it to the Lord in prayer.
Do thy friends despise, forsake thee?
Take it to the Lord in prayer!
In His arms He'll take and shield thee,
Thou wilt find a solace there.

Blessed Savior, Thou hast promised
Thou wilt all our burdens bear;
May we ever, Lord, be bringing
All to Thee in earnest prayer.
Soon in glory bright, unclouded,
There will be no need for prayer—
Rapture, praise, and endless worship
Will be our sweet portion there.

Because I anchored my meaning in my relationship with God, I didn't
search for it in other places. I also didn't get totally overwhelmed by my
circumstances. It would have been easy to do so. Instead, as I began taking the burdens to do the Lord, one by one, not only did my friendship
deepen with God, but my burdens fell by the wayside, and peace became
my lot.

Satisfaction

The second thing I discovered was that Jesus had become an even greater source of satisfaction for me. One of the highlights of my life was to
be married to Michelle. I absolutely loved it. My natural tendency is to be
relational. I am usually very open and honest with people, sometimes to
a fault. However, this openness and honesty are what made our relationship so special, because Michelle responded to me in the same way. But

now, for the first time in 23 years, I was single. The companionship that my heart longed for was gone.

Despite my desire to be married, I knew not to rush into things and find someone too quickly. I must admit, however, that I laid awake many nights battling feelings of loneliness, particularly during the first six months. But I knew that singleness was my future at least for the time being, and probably for the foreseeable future. So I needed a source of satisfaction that didn't involve a mate.

I needed to be content and find my satisfaction solely in Jesus until the right woman came along. Instead of hurrying to marry the wrong person, only to regret my rashness later, I decided to wait for the right person and dedicate myself fully to kingdom work.

If I were to be married again, I needed someone with whom I could spend the rest of my life. So things like compatibility, chemistry, and commitment would all need to be present before I could commit myself to someone else. Marriage is a lifetime commitment, and I knew there would be no turning back.

Finding a suitable partner was just one consideration, however. My wife would also need to be a mother to Faith. God had given me Faith and inspired me to lay out a plan to equip her for adulthood. This plan included a mother's input. So any woman I considered for marriage needed to fulfill that role, as well.

Finding someone who can be a compatible partner and a mother to my elementary-aged daughter with special needs is a tall order. Then throw in the fact that I am not the most attractive man on the planet, and it was easy for me to conclude that finding the right person would take a little while. I needed to settle into the single life.

Thus, I needed to locate my satisfaction increasingly in Jesus. While you might be tempted to dismiss this as a tawdry Sunday school cliché, it is what Jesus offers to anyone who is willing to trust in Him.

Several years ago, a friend gave me a book, *Desiring God*, by John Piper,[42] that revolutionized my perspective on happiness. The central

---

42 John Piper, *Desiring God: Meditations of a Christian Hedonist* (New York: Multnomah, 2011).

thesis of the book is that "God is most glorified in you when you are most satisfied in Him."[43] I longed to be happy (and this was not a bad thing), but I needed to put Piper's thesis to the test by placing my happiness in something that would satisfy.

This meant realigning my focus from thinking I needed a wife to focusing on growing deeper in my relationship with Jesus. I needed to love God more than I loved being married. As Jesus invites us in John 6:35, "I am the bread of life; whoever comes to me shall not hunger, and whoever believes in me shall never thirst." What was Jesus saying here? He meant He is the source of satisfaction. He is the one who satisfies the deep longings of the soul. He asks us to reorient our loves. I needed to reorient my loves.

If I was to love God even more than I loved being married, I needed to make Jesus the "greatest source of [my] consolation, hope, joy and value."[44] I needed to "grasp and be gripped by the true story of God's actual sacrificial, saving love for us in Jesus."[45] So I meditated on the Scriptures that communicated these truths and asked God to illuminate my heart. The result? Jesus became an increasing source of my satisfaction. I replaced some old thought patterns that were in contraction to Scripture with ones that reflected these truths. This is called preaching the gospel to yourself. [46]

To reorient my loves, I needed to see Jesus as the greatest source of my satisfaction. According to Martyn Lloyd-Jones, much of our trouble stems from allowing our selves to talk to us rather us talking to our selves. So he advocated preaching the truths of the gospel to oneself. Finding my satisfaction increasingly in Jesus required me to wrestle with

---

43 See John Piper, God Is Most Glorified in Us When We Are Most Satisfied in Him," October 13, 2012, DesiringGod.org, *https://www.desiringgod.org/messages/god-is-most-glorified-in-us-when-we-are-most-satisfied-in-him*, accessed November 9, 2017.

44 Keller, 93.

45 Keller, 95.

46 See, for example, David Mathis, "Preach the Gospel to Yourself," April 5, 2014, DesiringGod.org, *https://www.desiringgod.org/articles/preach-the-gospel-to-yourself*, accessed November 9, 2017.

and dismiss old affections and thought patterns and replace them with new ones.

Have you realized that most of your unhappiness in life is due to the fact that you are listening to yourself instead of talking to yourself? Take those thoughts that come to you the moment you wake up in the morning. You have not originated them, but they start talking to you, they bring back the problem of yesterday, etc. Somebody is talking. Who is talking to you? Your self is talking to you. Now this man's treatment (Psalm 42) was this; instead of allowing this self to talk to him, he starts talking to himself, 'Why art thou cast down, O my soul?' he asks. His soul had been repressing him, crushing him. So, he stands up and says: 'Self, listen for a moment, I will speak to you'. Do you know what I mean? If you do not, you have but little experience.

The main art in the matter of spiritual living is to know how to handle yourself. You have to take yourself in hand, you have to address yourself, preach to yourself, question yourself. You must say to your soul: 'Why art thou cast down'—what business have you to be disquieted? You must turn on yourself, upbraid yourself, condemn yourself, exhort yourself, and say to yourself: 'Hope thou in God'—instead of muttering in this depressed, unhappy way. And then you must go on to remind yourself of God, Who God is, and what God is and what God has done, and what God has pledged Himself to do. Then having done that, end on this great note: defy yourself, and defy other people, and defy the devil and the whole world, and say with this man: 'I shall yet praise Him for the help of His countenance, who is also the health of my countenance and my God'.[47]

---

47 Quoted in Kevin Neil Sanders, "MLJ Monday | Preach To Yourself," February 16, 2015, *https://knsanders.wordpress.com/2015/02/16/mlj-monday-preach-to-yourself/*, accessed November 9, 2017.

What Jones describes as the path to being satisfied in God sometimes requires that we go through "a process of honest prayer and crying, the hard work of deliberate trust in God, and what St. Augustine called a re-ordering of our loves."[48]

Freedom

Third, I needed Jesus to become a greater source of freedom for me. However, to understand the freedom Jesus offers required that I define freedom properly. Since the hallmark of the United States is liberty, I needed to exegete my own culture to counter any misunderstanding of freedom I may have ingested from it.

This cultural narrative, of course, has been present throughout American history. Americans fought against the tyranny of British rule so they could be free. However, this notion has gone through a metamorphosis since that era. Robert Bellah, in his book *Habits of the Heart*,[49] says that America has embraced three types of individualism. The country began with civic individualism, in which people value freedom but also have a strong commitment to be good citizens for the public good.

This gave way to utilitarian individualism, in which philosophers such as John Locke saw the individual as more important than the community. In this system, people have the right as individuals to fulfill their material interests. According to Bellah, this type of individualism, in its purest form, meant that "in a society where each vigorously pursued his own interest, the social good would automatically emerge."[50] Millennials today, by and large, reject this approach.

Meanwhile, today's expressive individualism is inherently secular. This approach has dispelled all transcendent notions of right and wrong aa emanating from God. Instead, it centers on the idea that "[n]

---

48   Keller, Kindle Locations 3378-3379.

49   Robert N. Bellah, Richard Madsen, William M. Sullivan, Ann Swidler, Steven M. Tipton, *Habits of the Heart: Individualism and Commitment in American Life* (Oakland: University of California Press, 2007).

50   Bellah, et al., Kindle Locations 1071-1072.

othing ... has any rightful claim on us, and we may live as we see fit."[51] This is freedom in our contemporary society.

The Bible rejects this notion of freedom. God has set parameters on what we are free to do. However, our obedience is based on a love relationship with God. We *want* to obey Him because we love Him. By aligning our lives and choices to what God desires, we experience true freedom. As the Gospel of John affirms, "So if the Son sets you free, you will be free indeed" (John 8:36).

But what kind of freedom does Jesus offer? From the context of this verse, it's clear that Jesus is talking about freedom from the bondage to sin. According to Keller, "All this means that Christians, like someone newly in love, are enabled to see the will of God not as a crushing, confining burden but as a list of God's loves and hates by which we can please him and come to be like him."[52]

When Michelle passed away, I had to deal with a sin I had been avoiding for some time. The truth was, I was very overweight, and things had to change. I wanted to be around for a long time, especially for Faith. This called for altering my eating and exercise habits. This alteration went beyond just self-discipline. It also required me to love God more than I loved food. I wasn't free to do just anything I wanted. It wasn't wrong to enjoy good food. It *was* wrong to eat to the point of harming my body. This was sin—and I wasn't free to do that. Through diet and exercise, though I still have a ways to go, I have lost about 60 pounds since Michelle passed away. This is real freedom.

Identity

The fourth thing I found was identity. We all have an identity. I do. You do. We all do. Since that question has been settled, two more questions still need to be asked. The first one is obvious. What exactly is meant by identity?

---

51 Keller, 99.
52 Keller, 114.

In short, identity is who you are. But who gets to decide? Keller often points out that identity formation in modern cultures means the individual gets to decide, making the individual the source of his or her own identity.

Traditional society's identity formation, on the other hand, is collectivist. One's identity is shaped by the needs of the community over and above the needs of the individual. Social roles are defined by putting the community's needs before one's own. Since families are viewed as the building block of society, then following pre-determined gender roles within the family structure is much emphasized if not outright demanded. Therefore, a woman's identity might be rooted in being a good mother, so she subordinates her desire for a career for the good of the family.

Christianity, on the other hand, provides a third alternative identity source, one that is centered in the person and work of Jesus Christ.

When Michelle passed away, I lost the role of husband. I loved that role. I no longer had someone to lead, serve, care for, or love unconditionally. I had enjoyed pouring myself out to her. Now she was gone. This took a toll on me at first. It was difficult to adjust. At 8 p.m., I put Faith to bed. For the next 4 hours until I retired at my usual midnight bedtime, I did a lot of thinking, mostly about the future. When you are married as long as we were, it is difficult to remember what life was like before you were married. For me, it was like another lifetime.

Soon, my identity as a parent began to waver. I fulfilled the role of dad well, but now I was asked to take on another role, that of mom. I had to do the things Michelle used to do. In contemporary society, the concept of gender has changed dramatically. People used to understand that the two sexes were different, not just biologically but ontologically. God had designed the sexes in certain ways so that each could contribute to family life. But in recent years, more and more people have come to believe that gender is an artificial social construct.

For the first time, I felt inadequate as a parent, which propelled me to deepen my understanding of my identity in Christ. To be *in* Christ meant that I was united *with* Christ. Therefore, I had His righteousness. I was totally accepted and completely forgiven. I am His. This means I am eternally accepted in the beloved. This is where I am to locate my identity. I am primarily a child of God.

Hope

Fourth, I had to locate hope. Throughout the Bible, we see men and women whom God brought through adversity. People like David, Jonah, Moses, Abraham, Sarah, Deborah, Paul, Peter, and even Jesus Himself come to mind. For the believer, tough times do not mean absence of joy and contentment, because Jesus is where one finds contentment. As He said, "I have said these things to you, that in me you may have peace. In the world you will have tribulation. But take heart; I have overcome the world" (John 16:33). We can draw three things from this passage: (1) Jesus planned for us to have peace. (2) You and I will experience troubles in this life. (3) Trust God in the face of adversity. How does one do this?

I spent many nights claiming the promises of God as I fought loneliness, despair, and depression. One evening, I stumbled onto a song called *Though They Slay Me*.[53] The song speaks of how, in the face of a tragedy, the believer should trust God. Why? Oddly enough, because he or she can know God better. One phrase in the song that pierced my heart said, "Though you take from me, I will bless your name."[54]

At the end of the song, a one-minute snippet of a John Piper sermon comes on. Piper is reflecting on a passage found in 2 Corinthians:

So, we do not lose heart. Though our outer self is wasting away, our inner self is being renewed day by day. For this light momentary affliction is preparing for us an eternal weight of glory beyond all

---

53 See https://www.youtube.com/watch?v=qyUPz6_TciY.
54 Ibid.

comparison, as we look not to the things that are seen but to the things that are unseen. For the things that are seen are transient, but the things that are unseen are eternal (2 Cor. 4:16-18).

As I reflected on it, this Scripture infused an incredible sense of hope in me. It reminded me not to lose heart and provided several contrasts between my current state in life and eternity. The resurrection of Jesus Christ made each of these contrasts a reality for me.

First, though I am getting older as "my outer self is wasting away," my inner life is increasingly being transformed. My outer life pertains not just to my body, but my mind and emotions. The despair I felt was just part of a temporal struggle. I am assured that when Jesus returns, "he will wipe away every tear from [my] eyes, and death shall be no more, neither shall there be mourning, nor crying, nor pain anymore, for the former things have passed away" (Rev. 21:4). This is the hope of the resurrection.

When I say "hope," I mean it in the biblical sense. Hope is not wishing. Hope is assurance. I can be *sure* that what I am going through now is temporary. It does not define my existence. My faith is squarely in the One who has died for my sins and been resurrected.

While my body is wasting away, my inner life is being renewed daily. The trials I am going through are part of my transformation process. This process can be expedited based on how I respond. As I resist the temptation to feel sorry for myself, and instead meditate on Scripture and engage in worship, God will transform me into the person He desires me to be. My difficult experiences drive me to anchor my hope more deeply in the finished work of Christ.

Thus, because of my future reality, I am to look "to Jesus, the founder and perfecter of [my] faith, who for the joy that was set before him endured the cross, despising the shame, and is seated at the right hand of the throne of God" (Heb. 12:2). What I am going through is temporary, light, and meaningful. This is the hope of the believer.

I had to reorient how I thought about life. Contrary to what many in American Christianity believe, God does not promise the American dream. I was not promised the middle-class, suburban life that includes a wife, 2.5 kids, and a white picket fence.

I may find myself 30 years from now having never found a wife. Faith may grow up without another mom. But whatever the circumstance, I am daily to be renewed in my relationship with Christ. If I continue to be renewed with God, I will be a transformed person.

Instead of lamenting the fact that I didn't remarry, I will praise the One who sustained me those 30 years and rejoice because I have grown closer to Him. I will have lived out God's dream for me, one that far outweighs the American dream. I will have gained a slice of heaven while living here on earth. I will inherit contentment and peace from my experience. Jesus is my treasure. In him do I trust.

Let me end with an insight from Malcolm Muggeridge, a British journalist and satirist who eventually found Christ. He summarizes a spiritual quest that resulted finding ultimate fulfillment in Jesus Christ.

I may, I suppose, regard myself, or pass for being a relatively successful man. People occasionally stare at me in the streets – that's fame. I can fairly easily earn enough to qualify for admission to the higher slopes of the Internal Revenue – that's success. Furnished with money and a little fame even the elderly, if they care to, may partake of trendy diversions – that's pleasure. It might happen once in a while that something I said or wrote was sufficiently heeded for me to persuade myself that it represented a serious impact on our time – that's fulfillment. Yet I say to you – and I beg you to believe me – multiply these tiny triumphs by a million, add them all together, and they are nothing – less than nothing, a positive impediment – measured against one draught of that living water Christ offers to the spiritually thirsty, irrespective of who or what they are.[55]

It has been my experience that Jesus never disappoints.

---

55   Quoted in https://www.dailychristianquote.com/malcolm-muggeridgc-2/.